Taming Artificial Intelligence

Mind-as-a-Service: The Actionable
Human-Centric AI Blueprint for
Individuals, Businesses, & Governments

Brian Ka Chan

BOOK ISBN-13: 978-1-7751440-0-7
BOOK ISBN-10: 1775144003
E-BOOK ISBN-13: 978-1-7751440-1-4
AUDIO ISBN-13: 978-1-7751440-2-1

DEDICATION

To my wife Jessica, mom Kitty, and dad Fai.

CONTENTS

**Part: 5 MIND-AS-A-SERVICE AI
CLASSIFICATION**

Part 6: TAMING ARTIFICIAL INTELLIGENCE

PART 1

THE AI EVOUTION

CHAPTER 1
WHAT IS MIND-AS-A-SERVICE?

With Artificial Intelligence, we are
summoning the demon. - Elon Musk

Alberto is pushing through the crowded sidewalk, taking another bite from the tuna sandwich his wife prepared for him that morning. It's the third time this month that he had to leave his friends midway through lunch and rush back to the office. As soon as he gets back in and reaches his desk, he hears an alarm sound just above his tiny cubicles. Great, just as he suspected: another stab in the back by Nora, his AI "co-worker".

As the creative director and lead artist for a top ad agency, Alberto's job is supposedly to help his clients grab the attention of their target market by creating eye-catching designs. But ever since Nora joined the company, his job has involved a lot less creating original work and a lot more fixing up what Nora creates for him. "Nora is amazing", Alberto admits. And she truly is: Nora can take the artful designs that Alberto creates and generate 20,000 variations that play around with colors, filters, tone, and she can even put them online and instantly test how the customers respond to them. Give her a few more days and Nora can produce 350,000 more improved variations, categorize them, arrange to have them tested online, and find out which one works best with which actual users based on time, location, or even mood!

It was fantastic at first. Nora enhanced Alberto's work, helped his company make a lot more money, and gave them a lot more credibility with clients who simply couldn't deny the kind of results their ads were getting.

But all that started to change five months ago when Nora got an upgrade from her manufacturer. Now, she can do a whole lot more, and the honeymoon period with her and Alberto is over.

Since the upgrade, every now and then, Nora will send out highly visual alerts to Alberto, to Alberto' boss, and even to Alberto' boss' boss, informing them that one of Alberto's designs didn't perform so well. Worse, she even tells them exactly why they sucked! Alberto's boss and his boss' boss both still think that the designs he creates are as beautiful and original as they have always been. But Nora will chime in to remind them that, while they are nice "Data is data, and it isn't personal." And, of course, Alberto knows it isn't personal, but he just can't bear the way he's being undermined.

It's one of those "friendly reminders" that Alberto got when he returned from lunch. Nora figured out that one of the cartoon characters Alberto drew for a campaign aimed at kids aged 7 to 13 just wasn't moving the needle much. Until that problem was fixed, it would cost the company $3,983.35 per day. Alberto is still the creative director, so he has the final say over which cartoon character they will use. But Nora's new update has already produced 23 alternative options Alberto can approve immediately, and listed the potential new income that each option will bring in. Alberto's job used to be creatively stimulating. Now, he's just becoming a rubber stamper, just giving his approval to designs based on the data that accompanies them. He knows his value to the company is diminishing and that his days are numbered. His boss knows this, too, and so does his boss' boss. They all know because Nora knows and Nora has been forecasting how much value the company would get from replacing him with her AI partner Norman. And that's why he couldn't stick around for dessert at lunch anymore, why he couldn't even stay with his friends for the whole meal – he had to get back to the office and find ways to prove his worth.

"Why did I approve of us bringing in Nora?" Alberto thinks to himself on his way home. "What did I do to myself? Creative jobs were supposed to be safe from AI!"

Everyone was singing the praises of AI back then. Even Alberto was cheerleading it, hoping to get an edge by becoming one of the industry's thought leaders and early adopters. He thought he was being a visionary, but now he just feels like he shot himself in the foot.

Sounds unreal? It's not science fiction; it's what will happen if you clash with AI unprepared.

Fear of the AI Future

"Artificial Intelligence is frightening!"
"Artificial Intelligence is exciting!"
"Artificial intelligence is our fourth industrial revolution!"
"Artificial Intelligence means the end of jobs."
We've all heard statements like these, but who is right? Could they all be?

These kinds of dramatic pronouncements are no surprise when we look at some recent developments in AI:

The University of Tokyo reported that Watson, IBM's cognitive supercomputer, has correctly diagnosed a rare form of leukemia in a 60-year-old Japanese woman.

Self-driving cars already have far fewer at fault accidents per miles than the average human driver. Researchers estimate that driverless cars could, by 2050, reduce traffic fatalities by up to 90 percent.

Google's Alpha Go can play the game of Go – a game once thought to be unwinnable by machines – better than top champions.

Artificial intelligence is not new to academics. We can trace AI research to a workshop held back in 1956 on the campus of Dartmouth College. Since then, it has populated countless science fiction scenarios throughout the 80s and 90s. And you just have to turn on the television or pull up a news site to see that there is no shortage of pundits sharing their opinions about AI and what it will mean for us and our society.

Research on AI has not stopped over the last six decades, and we've seen a dramatic acceleration in the last few years. The pace of the research has sped up because many of the machines that used to be found only in science fiction are now not only possible, but also cheap to develop and becoming reality.

AI is an umbrella term for many things. All software that includes a built-in logic are considered artificially intelligent. Anything that could be programmed can be considered AI. That might sound a little obscure, so to set a foundation for the rest of the book, we'll work with a definition of AI that is less academic.

"Artificial Intelligence is use of science and engineering (software or hardware) to create intelligent machines that can make and/or act on decisions that usually require organic intelligence."

If that sounds broad, it's because it is. It includes anything that can make a decision and is not a living organism! Notice that this sets a very low bar for intelligence: any decision-making that isn't simply random will count as intelligent. That's not a problem for the definition. In fact, that's how intelligence works for us, too. Human IQ has a range from 40 to 160 and it's the same with AI: the smart thermostat that adjusts according to the ambient temperature in the room is on the very low end, while chatbots that can fool you into thinking you're messaging with a human are far more sophisticated.

Even though AI feels new, this definition shows us that it's been around for a long time. Remember those little ghosts that chase your character around when you play Pac-Man? Are they artificially intelligent? Yes, they can tell where you are they always move toward you, can't they? That kind of awareness and decision-making is all it takes to make them AI.

Even though those little characters were ghosts, they were never frightening. So, why all the fear over AI now?

The fears are mostly because we are threatened by the new possibilities brought on by sophisticated AI machines. We worry that AI will do our jobs better than we can, that AI knows more than we do, that AI will do our work at far cheaper costs, and that, ultimately, AI will betray us, enslave us, or even exterminate the human race!

Fear of lost jobs to automated AI machines is one of the most common topics in the business news these days because we are afraid of a jobless future for most of us. We've already seen how intelligent machines have replaced many workers on the assembly line, and once artificially Intelligent Machines are smart enough they'll be able to take over work that we once thought secure. A world with AI lawyers, robot surgeons, and digital jazz musicians is no longer far-fetched, so it's no surprise so many are worried that we will lose our jobs and, along with them, our purpose in life and our ability to add value to our society.

Many of us are also afraid of losing control to something smarter than us but that we don't understand how it works. The machines will do the things we do, only faster, better, and more accurately. And since we don't know how they do it, we have no way to keep them in check or stop them from overruling us.

You might not know it from most of the media coverage, but not everyone is worried. There is also a sizeable group of optimists who think that far from being a threat, AI is the answer to our troubles, that AI machines will serve us forever and free us from unpleasant work and mindless drudgery. Pixar Animation Studios gave us a view of such a world in their 2008 film Wall-E. It depicts a future in which all humans have abandoned planet Earth and live on board a spaceship called Axiom. The Axiom's passengers have grown obese and feeble due to their overreliance on AI machines to do their every task and to care for them. If we use this technology more carefully, however, we might well see an automated future that frees us to live meaningful lives, rather than idle ones.

You might be wondering where I stand. I think either camp could be right. The outcome really depends on us, as a society. Think of climate change. If we do enough to reverse the damage and repair the environment, in 30 years, we and our descendants will be able to look back and see that – thankfully! – all the doomsayers were wrong. Since we didn't start early enough, however, we are bound to face some troubling consequences, and the doomsayers, much to their dismay, will be at least partly right.

We don't have to make the same mistakes with AI. I am in the school that human lives will be tremendously improved by the popularization of AI, and that there are many solutions we can apply to avoid doomsday scenarios like Skynet, the neural net-based conscious group mind and artificial general super intelligence system that features centrally in the Terminator franchise.

One of the reasons I'm writing this book is because there is so much literature and publications about AI, machine learning, and science fiction type predictions about the future, but none of it offers a way to solve the problems that come with it. It seems so many people have the confidence it takes to speak on the subject, but no one has the courage to propose practical solutions.

And that's just what I intend to do. I am proposing a solution to Tame Artificial Intelligence.

The Opportunity

This is a book about our long-term future. Specifically, about how we can live in harmony with AI – if we start preparing now. Think of this as the AI version of the climate change proposal we should have received decades ago. It's not the same, to be sure, but it is a threat to the human race, and it is something we still don't know much about. We had been hearing about climate change for a very long time, but the problem was that we waited too long to take action. We weren't sure if it was real, we weren't sure if it would impact us, we didn't even know for sure what we could do to stop it. Somehow, we finally got country leaders' attention and they came together to sign the Paris Agreement, an agreement within the United Nations Framework Convention on Climate Change (UNFCCC) dealing with greenhouse gas emissions mitigation, adaptation, and finance starting in the year 2020.

The same kind of uncertainty surrounds AI. We have doomsayers, we have optimists, but we aren't yet entirely sure whether it is really a problem or not. As a strategist, I'm not interested in leaving our fate to chance. It's far better to address a problem (way) ahead of time and improve our response as time goes on. My aim is to convince you that this is the approach we should take: contain the risk of AI before it becomes real, and before it's too late.

But we don't need just any measure. We need a real strategy. With that in mind, I have started off with four criteria for an acceptable solution to the threat of AI:

1.   *Human First*: Humans and AI machines will seamlessly integrate and complement each other, allowing for optimal productivity rather than competing for scarce work.

2.   *Sustainable*: A long-term framework to minimize negative social impact by helping individuals and businesses transition smoothly from the current Weak Narrow stage of AI

to its coming Strong General stage.

3.   *Actionable*: Provides actionable plans from the perspectives of individuals, businesses, governments, and nonprofits or charities to secure a dominant place in the AI-driven future.

4.   *Fail Proof*: Allow some room for failure without catastrophic results, like AI turning against us and deciding to do us harm.

Taming Artificial Intelligence with Mind-as-a-Service (MaaS)

Mind as a Service (MaaS), is the outcome of a two-year "Human First" AI framework research project that seeks to maximize human productivity through a comprehensive understanding of operational methodologies, technology maturity models, product strategies, and detailed industry-specific opportunities. MaaS is practical because anyone can start planning, implementing and adopting it. It is universal because it impacts everyone, no matter your social role, whether you are a business leader, government official, employee, freelancer, parent, or student. MaaS is future focused with the present firmly in mind. The concepts may sound a bit ahead of our time, but I can foresee the practicality will arrive sooner than we think.

Mind as a Service (MaaS) is a Human-First Human-AI-Evolution framework that considers Artificial Intelligence as an evolutional extension to human capacities, reinforced by seamless Human-AI Mind integration.

MaaS is a framework that classifies and positions AI in our society. We have gone through similar frameworks as new inventions matured throughout history, just as we position animals (domestic pets vs. farming animals), guns and hammers (weapons vs. tools), and Tylenol 3 and Tylenol 1 (prescription drug vs. over-the-counter medication).

Human' = Human + AI

Seeing AI machines as an extension of human capacities means that Human = Human + AI. They are, in a lot of ways, like the cars we drive, which are really extensions of our legs designed to bring us from point A to point B more efficiently. As an extension of human beings, AI machines do not have rights or liabilities on their own, only the manufacturer or accountable owner do. They are, then, a lot like cars, which are only as safe as we are and that bear no liability for our use of them. This classification might not seem so urgent in the current, narrow stage of AI. But as we move from non-sentient artificial intelligence focused on single narrow tasks to artificial intelligences that can make larger critical decisions, this classification will become very important.

In order to control AI that is potentially smarter than us, we come to the part of MaaS concerned with the "seamless Human-AI Integration across intelligence, personality, and emotions." Essentially, by minimizing interactions and friction with our AI extensions, we can connect and integrate with the AI across various levels. The AI will become part of us, and our cognition and intellectual abilities will be extended by AI.

On the moral side, MaaS doesn't suggest that our AI extension will inherit all of our ethics and values. Instead, ethical restraints will be enforced through regulations, whether from industry or government.

That might sound strange at first, but it is essentially the practice we have been applying to everything from utilities to weapons and chemical substances. AI has impressive capabilities, but they are still objects and they will be classified as such in our ethical considerations.

The only difference between an AI machine and a hammer, a car, a gun, or a drug is that the machine is smarter and can make decisions on its own. Under the MaaS framework, regulation will be enforced by educating the AI.

Mind as a Service (MaaS) is a Human-First Human-AI Evolution

Many have characterized our coming future as an AI Revolution. AI, we are told, will overthrow the human race and take over the world, changing everything irreversibly. Thankfully, it is simply not true – or, at the very least, it is just an exaggeration. We don't want AI to replace us and enjoy life instead of us. We don't want a revolution that destroys our society. To prevent that kind of future, all we need to do is treat AI the same way we treat other human inventions, only with more care and safeguards. When cars were invented, we developed traffic laws to manage their use. Because we invented firearms, we also had to implement gun control laws. The only thing that makes AI different is that it's smarter. But that shouldn't be a cause of worry. It's still essentially an extension to our own intelligence. We don't compete with cars by trying to outrun them, and we shouldn't get discouraged when we lose to a machine that is built to be smarter.

What I foresee is not an AI Revolution but an AI Evolution. With MaaS, humans can evolve rapidly, skipping millions of years to acquire new skills, forms of intelligence, and advanced productivity by leveraging technologies. AI is to our brains as our cars are to our legs. Cars take us from point A to point B with extreme efficiency without us needing to wait for evolution to gift us with 10 pairs of legs. Likewise, AI allows the brain to extend its capacities and acquire, absorb, and interpret information for when we want it to and in the way we prefer.

Human-AI Evolution is the core concept of this book.

Mind as a Service Takes Sides – The Human Side

The MaaS model considers AI a tool —an extension to our capabilities, rather than something we just buy and own. MaaS-Intelligent-Agents (M.I.A./MIA for short, an intelligence artificial agent which could be a combination of software and hardware), will become a part of us, like a third arm or a second brain. However, instead of us learning, experiencing, or thinking of how to use this new tool, the tool will adapt itself to us. It will think for us. You heard that right: thinking for us! Not for itself!

In current technology and data analytics, the businesses that develop and maintain the intelligent services own the data produced or captured through them. For example, Amazon owns all your purchasing and browsing data, and they use the data to recommend products to you.

Call this the Outside-In model. It involves an external artificial intelligence pushing decisions and "recommendations" upon us. In these cases, the recommendation that you receive is bounded to the ecosystems of the company you are interacting with; they are not sharing across platforms and talking to each other. The AI who is "serving" you have hidden agendas. These corporate machines are smart and they don't reveal their agenda, but it is obvious if "they" have to choose a side, it won't be ours.

MaaS proposes a different philosophy, one that puts our most valuable machine age assets – our data, our control – back into our hands. The Mind as a Service model centralizes the AI's capabilities and gives us full control of our data and the decision to use it or act on it. It is an Inside-Out model.

There are a few immediately obvious advantages to this approach:
- Our decisions are not biased in favor of external parties
- Full control of decision-making capabilities
- Full control of data privacy

Rather than attempting to influence or manipulate our decision-making, AI guided by MaaS help us in our autonomous decision-making by saving us from the time it takes to think over and make choices about every small detail.

Your Mind at Your Service

An MIA will be like a cloned mind that helps me make daily decisions. As technology advances and our lives get more complicated, we do not want to spend much of our energy and brain power on things that are not productive to us. For example, when to wake up and leave home if we want to get the most amount of sleep while still making it to our 7:45 meeting with a full stomach. Your MIA would be able to figure out these details for you in real time and reassess the plan if the situation changes in any way. Instead of trying to decide when to set your alarm clock, it will free you up to worry about what to say in the meeting. Your MIA will know your history, character, and how you're feeling in the moment. Because of that, it won't force a decision on you but will make the same decisions you would, decisions that reflect your personality.

Other People's Minds at Your Service

MaaS-driven AI will know your personality but will also allow you to outsource your decision-making to someone else. Let's say you idolize Brad Pitt and want to have his style. With his permission, you (along with his other fans) could use your Brad Pitt MIA to make the same decisions he would. For example, you could walk into a clothing store and know exactly what outfits Brad Pitt would choose or endorse if he were there. As the model matures, you could even create a kind of panel of other minds to guide your decision-making. Imagine being able to get real-time advice from a think tank of people you admire!

Your Mind Provides Service to Others

The MaaS that follows you 24/7 will gradually get a better understanding of how you make decisions. As it becomes more sophisticated, you will be able to clone your MaaS agent and outsource it to your employer, who can then leverage have you make decisions and interact with customers through your MIA. You might be wondering why an employer would go through the trouble instead of simply getting a generic AI machine to do the tasks. The key here is that every MaaS is unique and has a with different character, just like us. Our MaaS will be valuable to employers because everyone wants to interact with different human beings. Our MIA clones will have a distinct personality that will add a personal touch in customer interactions. For example, a kind-hearted MIA can be hired as a service agent at Disney to serve. History shows us that our expectations only go higher as technology advances, and this will be no different. We will be asking for real AI — *AI that represent real people, not invented characters or fine-tuned algorithms.*

Augmented AI is the beginning of Mind as a Service

Like every technology, this will take some time. The technology and infrastructure have to be developed, and more importantly, we need a culture that will support MaaS architecture. The first step of Human Centric AI is to augment our intelligence with Human Centric Augmented AI. It also takes time for an MIA to learn our individual thought patters, personalities, and preferences. The tech sector is getting more familiar with artificial intelligence, machine learning, and data analytics. But we are still far from building machines that can learn from us in a very meaningful way, let alone make decisions for us. Over the course of MaaS's evolution, we will see it go through stages of complexity, and we will have the opportunity to adapt as it develops. In part 5 of the book, we will discuss in detail the different levels of MaaS AI capabilities.

Mind as a Service Is a Strategy to Reduce AI's Negative Impacts on Humans

The MaaS strategy is to achieve Human-AI harmony by seamlessly integrating Human and AI capabilities, with AI understood as an extension of the human. The MaaS strategy allows humans and AI to do what they do best, and reduce friction by minimizing the need for explicit communication between them. The approach is to do it from the beginning and prepare ahead. By designing and guiding AI so that it acts in partnership to humans, we will be able to extract all of the benefits it holds for us while minimizing its negative effects on us as individuals and collectively.

Mind as a Service Is a Framework for

Human-AI Integration

MaaS is a framework. And as a framework, it is an abstraction, a concept, but one with definitions and references that can serve as guidelines for a harmonized and seamless integration of human capacities and AI technologies. Seamless integration means minimizing the interactions required between the human agent and their AI extension. A voice command is an interaction, a report on option is an interaction, a mouse click is an interaction. Each of them introduces some effort, some friction, in the use of AI. To make the integration successful, we have to make the process smooth by removing as many of these interactions as possible.

A qualifying MaaS Intelligent Agent (MIA) is an AI agent that consists of four critical capability dimensions:

• *Par or Super Human Intellectual Abilities*: the useful intelligence to make better than human intelligent decisions
• *Preference/Character/Ethics Capabilities*: the personal character, preferences, ethics, and worldviews that mirror those of the human agent
• *Emotional Capabilities*: the emotional information that informs the MIA of our mood, feelings, and preferences at the time of decision
• *Inspiration Capability*: the ability to dream and grow us to maximize our value to people we love, or the to our society

Not all AI require each of these capabilities, but a mature MIA will need at least three. Intelligence, character, and emotion is what will allow them to fully integrate with us –and a special inspirational capability will make the union complete.
Each of these are very distinct capabilities of our own minds, and each require different types of data to support informed and personal decision-making. All of them playing together will provide the major reference point that will allow machines to think the same way we do, based on our reasoning

patterns, personality traits, and emotional states. Taken together, they are a powerful replica of our state of mind and are well positions to make the best decisions on our behalf.

Par or Super Human Intelligence Capabilities

For something to qualify as a meaningful extension of human capabilities, it has to do something we do as good or better than we do it. A hammer, for example, hammering in a nail far better than our bare hands could. A car can achieve speeds that even our faster sprinters could never beat. A printer can write script more nicely, quickly, and consistently than the human hand. All of our tools add value in this way. Artificial intelligence's value is to be more intelligent than we can be. For example, a self-driving car is useful because it can make better driving decisions than we can. If the self-driving car drives worse than the average human being, no one will delegate their driving to the AI and expect to arrive safely at their destination.

When we apply the intelligence capabilities to MaaS, these capabilities work for us, instead of working for someone else, including corporations. That includes many of the commercial services we've come to expect. MaaS will, for instance, shop for the best products based on a personal history of purchases across all web sites, and maybe in physical stores.

Intelligence capabilities are the easiest to obtain. As a matter of fact, the industry has already accomplished early successes with Narrow Artificial intelligence. In 2017, Google's AlphaGo accomplished a difficult task, one that was once thought impossible: winning a game of GO against the global champion, Ke Jie. This is a great example of how narrow intelligence AI can excel at well-defined, rule-bounded tasks (we will consider MaaS's intelligent capabilities in greater detail in Chapter 7).

Having the best information and solid logic, however, are not enough to take over our decision-making. Each of us is unique, just like everybody else. What distinguishes us as individuals is the way we process information, how we think differently. The way we think in different situations is our character. For MaaS to be able to accurately make decisions on our behalf, it must, therefore, have Character Capabilities.

Preference Profile and Ethics Capabilities

Character capabilities refer to our personal character. Quite simply, it refers to how we think and the ways we behave across situations, our preferences for various things, and what we like and what we hate in general. Our character is usually very stable, unless we experience a dramatic shift in the way we think. Many of these characteristics can be identified through personality tests, such as the Myers-Briggs Type Indicator (MBTI). These tests do have limitations – much of it depends on how long your attention span is and how many questions you can answer. As a result, it is somewhat crude, resulting in only 9 categories of personality, which entails generalizing about the personalities it identifies. MaaS, on the other hand, can continue to learn from your behavior and adapt to your character and tendencies. Understanding what personality trait you have is easy; turning that into a decision model to make decision for you is going to be difficult. The personal character and ethical capabilities are also the controls we have in place to ensure that our MIAs don't go rogue or cause harm.

Mind-as-a-Service is all about becoming a better you.

Once your MIA has analyzed your character, it will be able to make better decisions that align more closely to your preference and values. But we still have more to consider when we make decisions. Our preferences are one thing, but we also make decisions based on our emotions —how we feel about something and how we react during different situations. To really simulate our decision-making, MaaS must have the emotional capabilities to take our emotions into consideration without having us consciously inputting information about our emotional states.

Emotional Interpretation Capabilities

Emotional Capabilities are the most complex factor in the simulation of our mind. In large part, that is because they happen in real time. Emotions represent the current state of mind in response to the internal sensory functions of the body including sound, temperature, and noise; predicting our mental state at a given moment based on experience; and external environment. One way of understanding this process is to liken it to programming a machine with our subconscious mind. Our decisions and actions are influenced by the subconscious mind. In a nutshell, it is how we react based on our emotional history and responses, as well as the current situation we are in. For example, one person could respond to a stressful situation at work by eating a lot of sugar foods, while another might feel the urge to punch something. By automating our decisions in these situation, the MIA will be able to make you a better person by helping you control your emotions and fine-tune your reactions.

Mind as a Service is all about addressing your desires.

Inspirational Capabilities

Mind as a Service is maybe the first AI research program that talks about AI being inspirational. As our MIA become smarter than us, know our preferences, learn our limits, and anticipate how we would react emotionally – our loyal MIA will also become intimately familiar with our weaknesses. Its inspirational capability will work to improve on those areas of weakness by planning for us, looking for inspirational ideas, and even schedule time to learn a new skill.

Mind as a Service is all about becoming your better self.

Mind as a Service is a B2C model of AI

Mark Cuban once said, "The first trillionaire will be

someone who masters AI."I think he's on to something, but more specifically, I believe that whoever can master the harmony between humans and AI will be the one with the trillion dollar idea. We do not want corporations to control the way we think by telling us what to buy, where to buy it, and when to buy it. Nor would we want self-driving cars to take us to places we did not choose to go. Having control is very important to us humans; it's in our nature.

The MIA is created to be loyal to us, on our side, and an extension to our abilities. That means the technology will be owned and purchased by regular consumers like you and me, not government or corporations. MaaS MIA on its own is its own class of AI, which is built with human-AI integration in mind, built for consumers, and built to maximize human productivity. Manufacturers and suppliers AI technology, then, will be Business to Consumer (B2C) companies.

Mind as a Service creates a new class of advanced consumer products.

Mind as a Service builds your personal think tank

Mind as a Service also means minds at your service, meaning it allows your loyal MIA to partner with other MIAs to form a think tank that works for you. If you need to pick a dress for your daughter's wedding, you can consult your MIA, but that won't get you very far. Your MIA, after all, reflects your own opinions and decision-making patterns and t won't be of much help when you need a way to get beyond these. Instead, you can also borrow your daughter's MIA, her wedding planner's MIA, and even hire a stylish celebrity's MIA. The MIAs can work together to form a "Artificial Intelligence Wedding Dress Committee" that will find you a dress that matches your preference, fits your body shape, meets your budget, and that everyone else would like.

Mind as a Service multiplies minds.

Mind as a Service (MaaS) is the next employment class

Once technology advances enough that our MIAs integrates with us and efficiently thinks for us; once our MIA can integrate with other MIAs to provide combined values; and once our MIA acquires multiple intelligences and connects them, then we can hire it out to companies to work for us! By design, an MIA belongs to us. Just like the IPs we own, we can license our MIAs to companies and have them making money for us without us having to lift a finger.

Mind as a Service multiplies service qualities and income opportunities.

Mind as a Service (MaaS) is the next investment vehicles

Once our MIAs are able to work on our behalf, they become income-producing investments. The more powerful the value the MIAs can create, the more money we can earn through them. Think of it as a replicate of yourself: the more you educate yourself and acquire skills and experience, the more marketable you become. Your MIA is the same, and that's why it can become a strong asset, and even your ticket to retirement.

Mind as a Service brings you financial freedom

Mind as a Service enforces ethics and protects you

MIAs will be bounded by regulations and ethical standards.

These are enforced by their personal character and ethical capabilities. Like every tool and every law we have governing them, we cannot stop people from creating bad AI. But we can, at least, have a system to protect ourselves.

Mind as a Service provides a fail-safe AI society

Mind as a Service is the ultimate achievement in user accessibilities and user experience

By so thoroughly integrating human capabilities and AI extensions, Mind as a Service is basically the ultimate invisible user experience and extremely accessible. The ideal of seamless integration minimizes the need for user interface. The next generation of user accessibility will be MIA accessibilities because all new products will be built to be easily consumed by MIAs.

Mind as a Service eliminates human bias and inspires.

Mind as a Service (MaaS) is not One Size Fits All

The Mind as a Service Human-AI partnership will allow us to accomplish many more things than we currently can. However, MaaS is not the only answer to the AI threat, nor a solution to all potential challenges with AI. Mind as a Service is not a One Solution Fits All model.

Not all AIs are created equal. In theory, it comprises anything from a basic speech workflow automation to a super intelligence like J.A.R.V.I.S. (Just A Rather Very Intelligent System), the highly advanced computerized A.I. developed by Iron Man Tony Stark.

Mind as a Service (MaaS) is an AI classification system

Mind as a Service has a classification system based on six different levels, ranging from basic narrow AI to Super Human, Strong General AIs into 7 different levels from no artificial intelligence to Artificial General Super Intelligence that is smarter than all of human intelligence combined.

We'll go into more detail about his classification in Part 5 of the book: The AI Classification.

Mind as a Service (MaaS) welcomes governance

Governance is also an important topic in AI. Think about gun powder. We didn't have to regulate gun powder or explosive until we figured out how to make them into weapons. Cars didn't need regulation until they were built to go above a certain speed limit. The same will apply to AI. Until they have acquired a certain level of intelligence, they don't pose a major, immediate threat and there is no point in regulating them or holding anyone liable. AI could, for instance, be equipped to make a decision that can have direct or indirect impact to a human's life or wellbeing without human intervention. Once that is possible, we will have reached the point at which AI needs to be regulated and owners need to be legally accountable. It probably needs another book just to talk about risks, but we'll take a look at this big topic in Chapter 24: Governance and Risks.

Do you have time to wait?

Neither businesses nor individuals have time to lose in the race to capitalize on the next frontier of industry.

As a business leader or individual, you can prepare ahead and avoid getting into a situation like Alberto's. If you are reading this book, I assume that you care about AI, and you care about your future. And you've found the right book, because now is not a time to "wait and see;" now is the time to lead and control.

What's Next?

In the rest of the book, I will take you through a mind opening journey through the concept of Mind as a Service and explore the critical components of a successful and efficient MIA. I will also provide you with guidelines to prepare for this inevitable wave in operating models that will be useful whether you are a member of the working class or a leader in a Fortune 500 corporation.

As AI and machines become more powerful and smarter, there will be growing concerns about privacy and data ownership. Data is the new oil, and whoever owns it will have an edge in the development of sophisticated AI.

Let the inspiration begin.

Taming Artificial Intelligence

25

PART 2

HISTORY, MYTHS, CLASH

CHAPTER 2
A BRIEF HISTORY OF AI

There is nothing new in the world except
the history you do not know.- Harry S
Truman

Part 2 sets the foundation for and explains the challenges and opportunities that arise from the clash between human and artificial intelligence. In Chapter 2, I will give a brief history of AI, explaining relevant terminology along the way. In Chapter 3, we move from AI's history to its future and discuss the potential clash between humans and the AI they've built. If you're already familiar with the history of AI and are well acquainted with terms like Deep Learning, Neuroscience, Cognitive Computing, Natural Language Processing, Weak AI, Strong AI, Narrow AI, and Artificial General Intelligence, feel free to skip this chapter and move right on to Chapter 3. Otherwise, I recommend reading Chapter 2 to find out just how we got here and get a primer on the important concepts surrounding the current state of artificial intelligence.

Defining Artificial Intelligence

For the purpose of this book, I define AI as follows.

*Artificial Intelligence is use of science
and engineering (software or hardware)
to create intelligent machines that can
make and act on decisions that usually
require organic intelligence.*

Any organic intelligence that can be exhibited through a combination of hardware and software qualify as AI. Some would generalize even further, claiming that anything able to make a decision is AI, since making a decision is an intelligent process that is created by human artificially. Since the bulk of this book will be concerned with sophisticated types of AI (often, types that do not even exist yet), we don't have to worry about classifying those marginal cases.

We will also be discussing the ways AI augment or enhance our capabilities. But it's not this enhancement that makes something an artificial intelligence. A bulldozer, for instance, extends human power and augments our ability to exert force, but it does not count as AI. Cars have extended human mobility by leaps and bounds, but it is also not an AI. Television has revolutionized our ability to communicate at a distance, bringing not only words or sounds, but also facial expressions, settings, and other visual cues that were absent in other media. Still, it is not an artificial intelligence.

To understand the range of artificial intelligence, let's run through a few examples — some simple, some advanced, and others downright scary.

A tiny machine that can look for honey in nature like a bee is AI. A small drone that can look for signs of living humans in the wilderness, perhaps as part of search and rescue operations, counts as AI. So does a similar drone that looks for living human beings but does so in order to detonate a small explosive device two inches above their head.

A thermostat that automatically adjusts the A/C based on your patterns of presence in the room is AI. A machined equipped with solar panels that rotates to ensure its surface is always facing the sun is another form of AI. A machine that completely shuts off the heat at a South Pole research lab to converse energy is also AI.

A series of machines that can assemble a car without human intervention is AI. A machine that tests and identifies design flaws is AI as well. A machine that determines that the best way to increase passenger safety is to install guns or small rocket launchers on cars (allowing drivers to blast away obstacles before crash) is also AI.

The spellchecking or auto-correct software that fixes your spelling without you asking it to is AI; The same software using its capabilities to rephrase all bad news so that it has a positive spin is AI. Software that uses a similar process to create fake news in order to create conflict between targeted parties is also AI.

A video game character programmed to chase down your character is AI. So is a real robot that is programmed to chase you down in real life.

A car that makes sure you never drift outside of your lane is AI. A fully autonomous car that can drive by itself without any help from you whatsoever is also AI. A car that decides to lock you in to keep you safe from a fire (and perhaps inadvertently preventing you from running into your burning home to rescue your children) is AI, too.

A robot that can locate a bomb planted in an airport without human intervention is AI. A robot that uses the same kind of algorithms to figure out the best place to plant a bomb so it will remain undetected until it detonates is also AI.

As we can see from these examples, AI can be built with

impressive capabilities. But whether those capabilities are used to improve our lives or place them under threat is still to be determined. Throughout the history of AI, we see excitement growing as its capabilities are enhanced. But each development brings uncertainty and worries, and never more so than now when AI is improving at an alarming rate.

Alan Turing

The history of AI starts almost 70 years ago. In 1950, the English mathematician and pioneering computer scientist Alan Turing wrote published "Computing Machinery and Intelligence" in the philosophy journal Mind. The paper would prove to be a perennial reference point in discussions of artificial intelligence.

Turing's paper asks the question "Can machines think?" Arguing that neither the word "think" nor the word "machine" can be defined in a way that clearly satisfies everyone, Turing suggests that we "replace the question by another, which is closely related to it and is expressed in relatively unambiguous words." Instead of debating definitions endlessly, Turing proposed a new criterion for machine intelligence: "If a machine acts as intelligently as human being, then it is as intelligent as a human being."

This gave us the Turing Test, which continues to occupy philosophers, logicians, and computer scientists. The test is simple: if we can converse with a machine and be fooled into thinking that we are conversing with a human being, the machine must be considered intelligent. This gave engineers and inventors a goal to strive for when creating artificial intelligences: passing the Turing Test became their mark of success.

The Dartmouth Conference

A few years later, in 1956, the Dartmouth Summer Research Project on Artificial Intelligence convened at

Dartmouth College in New Hampshire. The conference sought to find ways to "make machines use language, form abstractions and concepts, solve kinds of problems now reserved for humans, and improve themselves." While Turning proposed a test for artificial intelligence, this program set the blueprint for AI innovation. While the scientists who gathered for the Conference only spent two months at their workshop, their effort took AI out of the realm of theory and brought it into the realm of achievable, scientific progress.

Expert Systems

In the field of artificial intelligence, an expert system is a computer system that emulates the decision-making ability of a human expert. Expert systems are designed to solve complex problems by using reasoning that is represented mainly as if–then rules rather than through conventional procedural code.

Expert systems are divided into two subsystems: inference engines and knowledge bases. The knowledge base is a compilation of facts and rules, while the inference engine is the mechanism that applies the rules to known facts in order to deduce new facts. Inference engines can also include explanation and debugging abilities

For all their impressive capabilities, expert systems are somewhat static. They can make use of knowledge but that knowledge must be uploaded to it in the first place. It does not, in other words, acquire the expert knowledge on its own (other than what it can infer based on the knowledge it already has).

Game AI

Game-playing AI has been an area of AI research since its inception. Three of the first examples of AI are the computerized game of Nim, a checkers program by Christopher Strachey, and a chess program by Dietrich Prinz.

The open-ended nature of games makes programming capable robot opponents especially challenging. This is why many of the newsworthy developments in artificial intelligence have been gameplaying robots, from IMB's Deep Blue defeating the chess champion Gary Kasparov in 1997 to IBM's Watson computer defeating the reigning Jeopardy! champions in 2011.

Implementing AI into games was a significant advance in video game entertainment. Although AI are now routinely incorporated into video games, early video games like Spacewar!, Pong, and Gotcha were based on discrete logic and strictly allowed competition between players, without any AI features.

Government Interests

Governments have attempted to build AI, too. In 1981, the Japanese Ministry of International Trade and Industry set aside $850 million for the Fifth Generation computer project. Their objectives were to write programs and build machines that could carry on conversations, translate languages, interpret pictures, and reason like human beings. Unfortunately, the project was a failure, due to their choice of concurrent logic programming, poor CPU performance, and option for less modern technologies. The project was terminated a decade and $400 million (USD) later. Despite the failure, it does invite us to ponder speculative histories. What would the world be like today had this project succeeded? Although the project never met its ambitious goals, it did spark inspiration across the globe. Other countries responded to the Fifth Generation project by initiating comparable programs. The UK began the £350 million Alvey project. A consortium of American companies formed the Microelectronics and Computer Technology Corporation (MCC) to fund large-scale projects in AI and information technology. DARPA responded as well, founding the Strategic Computing Initiative and tripling its investment in AI between 1984 and 1988.

Insect -like Robotics

Nouvelle artificial intelligence is an approach to AI pioneered in the 1980s by Rodney Brooks, then part of MIT's artificial intelligence laboratory. Nouvelle AI differs from classical AI by aiming to produce robots not with the intelligence of humans, but with intelligence at levels similar to those of insects. Nouvelle AI researchers believe that intelligence can emerge organically out of simple interactions with the real world, instead of the constructed worlds that are typically programmed into symbolic AI.

A competing approach, the behavior-based robotic approach, sets itself apart from traditional artificial intelligence by using biological systems as its models. Classic artificial intelligence typically uses a set of steps to solve problems, following a path based on internal representations of events. Rather than using preset calculations to tackle a situation, behavior-based robotics aims for adaptability.

Intelligent agents

In artificial intelligence, an intelligent agent (IA) is an autonomous entity that uses sensors to observe its surroundings, acts upon its environment, and exhibits goal-directed activity. As an agent, it is capable of acting upon information it perceives; as an intelligent agent, it can make decisions based on experience. Some IAs are also autonomous, meaning that they are free to choose from different sets of actions, rather than requiring human guidance. While we find this kind of intelligent agency throughout the wild, artificial IAs are those that are of special concern to those developing and studying AI. However, since "artificial autonomous intelligent agent" is quite a mouthful, the convention is to simply shorten it to "intelligent agent" or "autonomous agent," with the understanding that these refer to artificially created agents only.

Machine Learning

In layman's terms, machine learning refers to algorithms that change the way they behave in response to new data. For example, instead of telling a machine to stop at a red light, a machine learning algorithm can gather information and learn that red lights mean stop and that running one would be imprudent. Machine learning has been excitedly bandied about in popular media and hyped as the best thing since sliced bread. It is, however, only one of the many fields of computer science that give computers the ability to learn without explicit programming.

Machine learning is related to computational statistics, which also focuses on computer-based predictions. It has strong ties to mathematical optimization, an area of research and practice devoted to bringing methods, theories, and application domains to the field. Using the red-light example again, the computer can analyze a pool of data and learn that running a red light is far more likely to result in an accident than stopping and waiting for it to turn green.

There are many different approaches in machine learning, some popular ones including Decision Tree Learning, Artificial Neural Network, Deep Learning, Clustering, Bayesian Networks, and Reinforcement Learning. I won't go into too much detail about these, but I will devote some space to Deep Learning since it has been so popular in the media.

Deep Learning

Deep learning (also known as Deep Structured Learning or Hierarchical Learning) achieves recognition accuracy at higher levels than were previously possible. Deep learning has grown in popularity recently because the two things that are required to make it work are becoming cheaper now: data and processing power. Popular software applications and the Internet of Things ensure that vast quantities of data are constantly being generated and collected. Deep learning AI use these vast stores of labeled data as a reference when training. And the processing power is achieved thanks to the advent of cheaper high-powered CPUs, enabling deep learning processes to move at a much faster speed.

Deep learning is used in wide range of applications. Deep learning enables driving AI to automatically detect objects such as lanes and traffic lights. Medical researchers can use deep learning AI to detect cancer cells. It is also used in customer service, to automatically translate speech and retrieve information.

Most of deep learning methods use a neural network with multiple layers – anywhere from two to three hidden ones, all the way up to 150 layers (the most elaborate neural network architecture at the time of writing). The more layers, the better the AI's ability to learn complex ideas and contexts. In the very near future (within a decade, by my guess), we will have access to many deep learning AI with narrow but superhuman capabilities, like the one displayed by Google's AlphaGO, which can outplay humans at the game of GO.

Narrow AI

Narrow AI (or Weak AI) is artificial intelligence that is focused on a single narrow task. It is the only form of AI that we have achieved so far. The term is typically used to refer to a specific type of artificial intelligence that is able to match or outperform humans in some very narrowly defined tasks. This is the kind of artificial intelligence exhibited by the AI that is capable of surpassing human champions in chess, GO, or on the gameshow Jeopardy!.

Narrow AI is also used to make purchase suggestions, sales predictions, and weather forecasts. Outside of their narrowly defined domain, however, they cannot match human intelligence, let alone surpass it.

In some industries, narrow AI is frequently associated with the concept of automation. I consider automation as a synonym for AI because any machine or algorithm that can act on behalf of a human is an artificial intelligence by my definition. Automation, however, tends to connote simpler tasks, such as routing mail packages. While I do think the meanings are equivalent, "automation" may seem like an inadequate term once we get to discussing the future capabilities of advanced AI.

Artificial General Intelligence

General AI (also known as human-level AI or strong AI) is artificial intelligence that can understand and reason about its environment just as a human would. General AI has always been elusive. For decades, futurists have been proclaiming that it's just around the corner. Humans might not be able to process data as quickly as computers, but we can think abstractly and plan, solve problems at a general level without needing to dive down into the details, and innovate to come up with ideas that have no precedence. Think about the invention of the telephone, ships, telescopes, mail systems, social media, gaming, and virtual reality. AI is very efficient at performing routine tasks, but it's very hard to teach a computer to invent something that isn't already there.

If Artificial General Intelligence sounds outlandish or futuristic, it's because we are still very far from achieving anything close to it. We're still struggling to make AI that can do one thing better than humans, and most of our AI are simply able to automate tasks that involve only a very limited set of variables.

Some theorists posit that there is an even bigger obstacle to achieving AGI, namely, that it would require machines to achieve consciousness. Personally, I don't think a machine has to be conscious in order to have general intelligence. Just because we humans have both consciousness and this multifaceted form of intelligence does not mean conscious is a prerequisite to have general intelligence .

Artificial Superintelligence

According to the AI expert Nick Bostrom, once AI becomes much smarter than the best human brains in practically every field – including scientific creativity, general wisdom, and social skills – we will have invented an Artificial Super Intelligence.

Learning computers that can rapidly become super intelligent may take unforeseen actions or out-compete humanity. Researchers have feared that, by way of an "intelligence explosion" sometime over the next century, a self-improving AI could become so powerful as to be unstoppable. This is true, in theory. There is, however, one big assumption at the heart of this doomsday scenario: that humans will do nothing to prevent it. I doubt that we will simply sit on the sidelines and patiently put up with such a takeover. If we act early enough, we will be able to do something about it. This book is my attempt to do something. I am more concerned that we wait too long before we do anything to stop this kind of scenario from unfolding than I am about the technology simply marching forward. To me, that kind of progress is a given, not a question. The question is "What are we going to do about it?"

Now that we have gone over the history and some important concepts in artificial intelligence, we are ready to tackle concerns about AI. In the next chapter, I will answer some of the questions about AI that come up in popular media.

CHAPTER 3
THE MYTHS, THE CLASH, AND THE MESSY MIDDLE OF AI

Beginnings are always messy. - John Galsworthy

In this chapter, your will learn about:

• Myths about AI and the supposed coming clash between humans and machines

• The chasm between present technology and artificial superintelligence

• The messy middle on our way to that future

I will adopt a different format for this chapter. Unlike the rest of the book, I will present it as a Q&A in which I respond to common concerns, questions, and myths surrounding artificial intelligence.

What kind of impact will AI have on us?

It's difficult to know for sure exactly what the impact will be, but it clearly has the potential to be devastating. Stephen Hawking has repeatedly declared that the emergence of AI could be the most catastrophic development in human history. As Dr. Hawking states, "Unless we learn how to prepare for, and avoid, the potential risks, AI could be the worst event in the history of our civilization. It brings dangers, like powerful autonomous weapons, or new ways for the few to oppress the many. It could bring great disruption to our economy."

Elon Musk has also sounded the alarm about artificial intelligence in an open letter to the United Nations. In his letter, Musk indicated that the race to develop more advanced AI will eventually trigger World War III.

Are they for real? Do we really need to worry about AI?

Unfortunately, the answer isn't a simple "no."

If you are talking about the AI you see on the news and the devices that are currently being developed or hitting the shelves, then the answer is a resounding no. I am not concerned about any of the AI that you see featured on the news.

But I do find myself in some agreement with Musk and Hawking. While I see no immediate threats, I do see imminent ones. If we take a longer timeframe and look about 30 years into the future, then yes, we should worry about AI.

In fact, timeframe is at the heart of the debate. The main point of disagreement between the camp that views AI as dangerous (the camp I fall into) and the camp that thinks AI is too dumb to be worth taking seriously as a threat is the question of when things will go wrong, not whether they will. The latter camp is right to have no concern over the AI that are currently available to us. These technologies can only do so much, so we still have complete control over them. But if we're talking about the future when AI has learned to identify problems, frame issues, invent solutions, and make decisions entirely without human input, then we all have reasons to be worried.

Imagine a future in which we are under the thumb of a powerful, superintelligent dictator whose main objective is to not only make the trains run on time but to make everything on the planet efficient and to eliminate as much waste as possible. It becomes clear to them that having so many humans on the face of the planet is one of the things that makes it so wasteful and inefficient. Not only that, but they have access to the deadliest weaponry available, and with the touch of a button can clear all of the "efficiencies" off the map.

Now, replace that dictator with a machine and we have a scenario that could plausibly play out once AI is advanced enough.

Is that kind of superintelligence possible?

In theory, yes. In practice? No one knows for sure.

This is like going back in time 3,000 years and asking someone if humans will ever fly. I am sure almost every single person you would encounter would say no because would be so unimaginable and farfetched. But somehow, 2,900 later we somehow figured out a way to do it. We can't physically fly, but we have invented machines that can fly and carry us.

So yes, it is possible. In fact, we're not in the same position as those incredulous people 3,000 years ago. We're more like the people who first learned that the Wright brothers invented a flying machine trying to take a guess at whether we will eventually build a plane that can fly across the ocean or carry dozens of passengers.

Is there nothing to fear from current AI, then?

We do need to worry about AI, but not about it being so

intelligent that it makes humans useless. If we ever become obsolete, it won't be in the near future.

But I am concerned that AI starts being used in the wrong places and will be much harder to control and stop. AI can exist in some physical form as a robot, but in many cases, it is simply an immaterial algorithm. That immateriality makes it hard to tell if something is AI-free, and it's harder for us to know how to interact with it. It's harder to detect and harder to understand. And that's the source of a lot of the fear surrounding AI: all the unknowns.

The biggest misconception about AI is a misunderstanding about intelligence. Many people believe that natural general intelligence is unidimensional, meaning that intelligence can be ranked and measured along a single linear dimension. The truth is that intelligence is multidimensional. And that makes a certain amount of intuitive sense. While we talk about IQ scores like they accurately reflect a person's overall intelligence, we also recognize that just because someone is better at something than we are, it doesn't necessarily mean they are more intelligent. To drive this home, consider the following comparison. A frog might have a brain as little as 30 grams, much smaller than an average adult human brain mass of 1,350 grams. Considered as a whole, humans have a significant brainpower advantage over frogs. But then how can a frog with such a small brain be so fast at catching a fly? The tiny frog brain can locate a fly, track it, mobilize its tongue, and deploy it to capture the fly in less than a second. Although we have much more brainpower, when it comes to these specific tasks, we're no match for frogs. We can think of the frog as possessing superhuman intelligence in the domain of tracking and catching flies. The frog's brain is optimized to do one thing and to do it well, which is to watch the sky for any food that may be floating around. However, a frog's intellectual abilities are quite limited and strictly defined; it would starve to death if it were surrounded by dead flies, ready to be eaten but going unnoticed by the frog's brain.

Should we be worried that frogs will take over the world

because it can do something our brains can't? I would be surprised if anyone lost any sleep over this hypothetical frogpocalypse. Likewise, when we turn on the television and hear that machines are now becoming smarter than humans, I don't run to unplug my computer in terror. Machines can, indeed, do some things better than we can, but even the most powerful ones can only do a few narrowly defined tasks. Although none of them are busy catching flies, they basically surpass us in a narrow domain of intelligence just like frogs do. Besides, machines have long been better than humans at various things. How many of us can process a calculation as fast as a calculator? Yet are we terrified that calculators will make us obsolete somehow? No, and far from worrying about them, very few of us would want to live without access to calculators.

But the AI can learn now, so is it just a matter of time before they take us over?

Yes, machines and AI will learn more and more, there's no doubt about that. As AI develops, it can perform more narrow tasks better than humans can, and humans will not be able to compete with them – at those specific tasks.

Let's dip into the animal kingdom again for more examples. Birds can fly and we can't (not without the assistance of some very complicated machinery, anyway), lions can hunt in with speed and strength that put every human to shame, monkeys can climb trees faster than even the most agile human could ever hope to. Name just about any human ability and there is an animal out there that surpasses us in that domain. Should we worry about animals making us obsolete? Not unless they organize and band together to combine their strengths and overpower us. Likewise, just because more and more AI are developing individual superhuman capabilities doesn't mean they will be in a position to rule the world and make us irrelevant.

Couldn't an AI learn so well that it could master everything on its own?

For sure, but that would be very difficult and probably cost-ineffective. There is no business or organization in the world that can create so many technologies that they collectively replicate all human abilities. They may be very successful in small domains, with some of the best scientists and engineers in the world looking for ways to outperform others on a given task. And there's good reason for that: as the tasks get bigger and more varied, the results start to diminish. Entrepreneurs and corporate leaders now aim to build businesses that are agile, not just big, because we constantly see examples of super successful companies stop being innovative and having a difficult time adapting once they get bigger. Bureaucracies are complex, and that complexity makes the inefficient.

So, just because developers are building AI that are hyper optimized at fulfilling single tasks doesn't mean that they can just keep heaping capabilities on it and still get great results. Just like small businesses, it's precisely because the AI have such narrow capabilities that their performance can be so impressive.

What if there were an AI specialized in coordinating all of these different narrow intelligences?

Now that's a more interesting question. In theory, we could build a machine that has the intelligence to coordinate and orchestrate different scatter narrow AI so that they act as a collective unit rather than as scattered tools. The coordinating AI would be like an animal handler who trains and commands marine animals at a Marine Park: they can't swim gracefully, bark like seals, or do impressive leaps out of the water like dolphins, but they are able to get a pool full of animals to put on a majestic show. Likewise, this AI conductor would not need to have various capabilities, but only one: organizing and unifying the abilities of a group of narrow AI algorithms.

I am more worried about this kind of AI than I am about any of the ones we have seen so far. This AI would have to possess the type of intelligence we humans have used to dominate the Earth: problem solving. We haven't developed a problem-solving AI yet, but if we do, then we have cause to be a bit careful with how we use it.

AI conductors sound scary. How would we deal with them?

This question is one of the reasons I wrote this book. My answer is that the only way to tame any AI who has the ability to use many superhuman narrow AI is to design them so they only work for us, for our interests.

Have you heard of the decapitation strike strategy used in warfare? It's a long-standing tactic, and it works on the idea that if you eliminate military or political leaders, you can shatter or defeat the enemy. My idea is similar, but instead of eliminating the AI that is at the head of the collective, we partner with it, lead it, and retain control over it.

I'm not suggesting that any kind of conducting AI would necessarily harm humans, but AI functions are always in service of some goal, so we have to tame them to ensure that the goals are always human-centric. There is a risk that AI will not consider every consequence of their actions, or that they may not weigh seriously the kinds of considerations we think are paramount, so we need to remain in the driver's seat even while we're delegating more and more to AI.

The AI on a military drone's goal is to kill enemy, a stock-trading algorithm's goal is to buy and sell financial products to maximize earnings, an AI tasked with making a workplace more efficient's goal is to do as many jobs as it can and take human out of equation.

We should be scared when the goals are misaligned so the AI tries too hard and goes beyond what we would consider reasonable. If the weaponized drone's AI realizes that the best way to eliminate the enemy is to bomb an area indiscriminately, regardless of how many civilian casualties it will cause, fulfills its goal but not in a way that we would consider reasonable. Likewise, an AI tasked with making a workplace efficient could simply fire all human workers and leaders and take over its entire operations, but we would consider this to be a misstep, even though it would fulfill the AI's stated goal.

The only way we can prevent these things from happening is to tame the AI before it's too late and it can no longer be tamed. AI can be a beast that intellectually outguns humans, and the only way that we can control it is to start restraining it before it becomes too powerful.

You may have heard of the elephant on a stake story. Elephants are so powerful that training them seems like an insurmountable task. The way to work around this, of course, is to tame them before they become so powerful. Trainers will start when they are still small and tie a rope around their necks to keep them tethered to a secure pole. The baby elephant tries to walk away but is consistently stopped short by the rope. They'll pull and push and twist and turn but eventually they figure out that they just aren't strong enough to break free from their shackles, so they stop resisting and just stay where they are. It eventually recognizes the futility of fighting back and resisting. That is why giant circus elephants will stand passively when there's a rope around their necks, even if it isn't attached to anything.

AI will be smarter than an elephant, and it will be able to do calculations and figure out whether it can be controlled. But like the elephant trainer, our best hope is to tame the machine before it grows too strong. Just imagine trying to rope and control a fully grown, wild elephant. You and your rope won't stand a chance. It's the same with AI that once it grows too powerful.

What should we do to address the AI Threat?

Here's a brief checklist of things that I think we should be doing:

1. Stop worrying about the AI technologies we have now (they're the frogs and baby elephants who don't pose much of a threat)

2. Start worrying about the AI technologies of the future (the AI conductor, the superintelligent dictator)

3. Address the threat before it becomes powerful and unstoppable

4. Always stay one step ahead of the growing power

5. The easiest way to be a step ahead is by combining forces with AI, creating a Human + AI force that can't be easily overthrown

Sounds great. But how do we go about it?

The rest of this book will cover the concept and principles. I am going to introduce you to new ideas about AI and offer the first framework that helps us reposition the development of AI as a narrative about AI-assisted Human Evolution instead of an anti-human AI revolution. Some of the major concepts I will cover include

- Human-Centric Artificial Individual Intelligence
- AI-Assisted Human Evolution
- Human + AI as the best solution to combat AI Risks
- A New Mode for Human Capital
- How to "Build" the Human-AI Evolution

And much more.

47

PART 3

THE MIND-AS-A-SERVICE MODELS

CHAPTER 4
ARTIFICIAL INDIVIDUAL INTELLIGENCE - YOUR MIND AT YOUR SERVICE

Once a person is determined to help themselves, there is nothing that can stop them. - Nelson Mandela

---

"Seventy-two. Seventy-three. Seventy-four. Gosh, that's a lot of people."

Mark is counting the number of guests coming to his girlfriend Marvis's birthday party, where he's planning to ask the big question.

He volunteered to organize the party because he didn't want any chances of his proposal plan getting leaked. But now he only has less than two weeks to plan everything. It's not his fault he didn't remember her birthday earlier. Nor that he came to such a quick decision about proposing to her only two weeks before that. Besides, he couldn't have started planning any earlier because he was pulling in 20 hour days during the last week trying to finish the biggest project he'd ever worked on. With all that excitement, he just couldn't help feeling that it was a great time to propose and celebrate a big bonus.

"Ta-da!" A message notification interrupts his worried planning. It's a message from Marvis. "Jess is asking if I'm having a party this year. What should I say?!?!?!   WILL I?! >_< "

Now the panic really sets in! How is he going to find a venue that fits eighty people with only a two-week notice? Worse: he still hasn't bought the ring! And he doesn't even know where to start when it comes to picking a theme. Marvis likes nice surprises. He can't screw this one up.

"This is too much," he thinks. "Maybe I should just forget about it and propose another time."

But Mark isn't the type of person that gives up easily. There has to be a way. "I just need help. That's all."

And that's when he remembers the MaaS Intelligent Agent (MIA) he signed up for two months ago. He hasn't even turned it on yet because he isn't all that comfortable with the idea of a machine making decisions for him.

"Oh, what the heck! If it sucks, I can just delete it and no one will even know." He proceeds to activate MIA on his personal devices.

His own voice greets him from his smartphone. "Hey Mark! What can I help you with?" Mark decided to use his own voice for the AI agent when he signed up.

"I want to propose to my girlfriend Marvis next Saturday," Mark tells is device. "But I still have to find a venue for 80 people, I need to get a ring, and I have no idea what to do! What can you do for me?"

Fifteen seconds after Mark's explanation, the MIA reports back. "Easy. There are three venues that can house 90 people within 30 kilometers of Marvis's home. They all have a ten-person buffer and plenty of easy parking. One is funky, one is high end, and one is a dark and romantic restaurant. I think Marvis would like the dark and romantic restaurant —she often likes that kind of thing in pictures on social media. Here are some pictures of each location for you to check out. I have put in a fifteen-minute hold on all three places for you. "

"This place looks good," Mark exclaims. "Deal! just book it and handle the invitations and RSVPs. I am authorizing you to access the invitation list in my cloud drive. But what is the rundown?" Mark is pleasantly surprised by how easy all of this suddenly became.

"The rundown that will work for her and be easiest for you is an acapella band singing a selection of songs that hint at weddings and marriage in the lyrics. Here is a list of songs Marvis has recently listened to with the lyrics changed to add mentions of 'family' and 'marriage.' You just have to pay $50 for these lyrics and the copyright if you want to record it." And, just like that, another problem solved.

"Sounds good!" Mark feels productive already.

"Done. Your total cost for the night will be around $2,600 - $3,200 – about what you spent on Mavis' birthday celebrations the last three years."

"OK, great... But what about the–" The MIA interjects before Mark can finish asking the question. "–I've reserved three princess-cut diamond rings for you at a diamond wholesaler. They are the best deals I could find within your budget at the moment. I have already scheduled you to examine and pick one up on Thursday at 4pm, or exchange it for another one. I will let you know if I find better deals before then."

"OK. So, what else do I need to do?" Mark asked with some satisfaction –he could really get used to this.

"Nothing for now. I will let you know. Just don't turn me off so I can keep working. And remember that you have to call your boss in five minutes. Oh, and by the way, Marvis just saw the invitation and accepted it within 26 seconds. It looks like a good sign to me." The MIA then goes to work looking for better diamond ring deals for Mark, and Mark calls his boss, feeling like his upcoming marriage is already off to a good start. End.

In this chapter, you will learn about:

- Technological advancements in the history of organizational productivity, organizational-information explosion, organizational Data Intelligence, and organizational AI
- Basic Mind as a Service concepts, including:
  - Applying organizational AI technologies to amplify personal productivity
  - Loyal AI built to serve you, and only you
  - The extended human brain
  - The Human-AI Evolution

Before we focus on Mind as a Service, I will spend a few pages walking you through a brief history of technologies that might seem like they have no direct relationship to AI on the surface, but in fact played an important role in bringing us where we are today and explain how AI became trendy. Without this progression of technologies and the changing needs of the business world, we would not be in the prime time for AI.

I will start with the rise of organizational productivity, then move on to data intelligence due to standardized processes, to the early phase of using data-driven decision making, and to the early formation of AI methods such as machine learning. I will then describe how the same transformation will be applied to individuals, which will form the basis of Mind as a Service.

Organizational Productivity

The history I am tracing starts back in 1769. On that year, a gentleman named Richard Arkwright, credit as the brains behind the growth of factories, patented his spinning frame. The device spun thread mechanically, allowing each user to produce more than they could by hand. After patenting his spinning frame, he opened up the first true factory at Cromford, near Derby in Great Britain.

Arkwright's commercial enterprise would soon change Great Britain. Before long, his factory employed over 300 people. In an economy driven by craftsmen and workshops, nothing on this scale had ever been seen before. The domestic production system only needed two to three people running a small cottage industry from their own homes. By 1789 – two decades after Arkwright's patent – the Cromford mill grew to 800 workers. Operating the machinery was fairly simple. So, with the exception of a few engineers, the bulk of the factory's workforce was essentially unskilled. While workers in the domestic system could set their own hours and enjoyed some degree of flexibility, the factory's employees were assigned a job to do over a set number of hours. In Arkwright's mill, set procedures and the hands of the clock governed the workers.

Soon after, Edmund Cartwright's power loom entered the scene and ended the lifestyle of skilled weavers. In the 1790's, weaving was a well-paying job. But within 30 years, machines had taken over the tasks and many weavers had to become laborers in factories. The productivity gains were appealing to industrialists and the machinery took off. In 1813, there were only 2,400 power looms in Britain. By 1850, there were 250,000.

Fashion, Infrastructure, Processed Food, Scaled Manufacturing

The same advancements in organizational productivity transformed other industries and organizations during the Industrial Revolution.

The sewing machine was invented in the 19th century and streamlined clothing production in the textile and industry. Cars were invented in early 20th century, making transportation a lot easier and cheaper. The large scale of production plants made manufacturing far more productive than it once was. As organizations became more productive, developed monitoring techniques, and standardized their processes, they began generating a lot of data and information. A standardized production line of processed canned food, for example, would have standardized procedures, uniform steps, and a quality control process. Each of these stages in the process from the supply chain to the shop floor could generate lots of data. Industrialists could carefully calculate time to ship, the time required to assemble, defected SKUs percentages, and sales data. All of this was then used by analysts to better understand the business's organization.

Organizational Business Intelligence and the Information Explosion

Standardized processes create a surprising amount of data, regardless of whether they are stored in an effective database or jotted down on paper. Data are collected and measured whether they are collected with a purpose or not. The last few years has seen an explosion in data collection and analysis. 90% of our available data has been collected within the last two years, and we are creating 2.5 quintrillion bytes of data every day. It is impossible for us to consume and understand all of this data. This problem has been around for businesses and other organizations since the 80s, when companies began to realize they need to manage their data in much the same way they manage their warehoused assets.

That's what started that decade's "data warehouses," which brought together disparate data sources and stored them in one place. It didn't take long for the value of data warehousing to become clear: it imposed some structure on something that is unstructured by nature. By centralizing and organizing accumulated information, data warehousing drastically cut the time it took to access data.

Business leaders and the tech industry came to realize that they needed to extend their data analysis capabilities in order to better understand their business operations. That marked the start of business intelligence (BI). But technology did not advance to the point where it could be considered an agent of business intelligence until the end of the 20th century.

Business intelligence platforms had undergone intense refinement in agility and speed in he mid-2000s. Tool specification, expanding self-service options, and improved visualization were three of the most important traits in this new frontier of the BI evolution.

We then entered the era of big data. Big data is considered the next generation of BI and data warehousing, except it claims to do more, and to do it faster and easier.

As big data analytics matures, our expectations grow along with the technology. We now have businesses that want to use the data to uncover the fine-grained details of their performance. There is also an increasing expectation that data will be the basis of many business decisions, including approving projects, creating new product, acquiring companies, and hiring and firing personnel. By combining the data they gather about their operations with external data like market data and social trends, companies can further strategize and make tactical, data-driven decisions.

As you may have guessed, the logical next phase of business intelligence is prediction and actionable insights. Thanks to technological developments like basic data reporting, BI visualization, machine learning, deep learning, and AI algorithms, data analysis has moved away from giving a static or historical picture of how a company is doing and is now providing recommendations for how a company could do better in the future. This predictive analysis essentially tell business leaders what they need to do to maximize returns for their stockholders. Increasingly, corporate actions like changing the price of an airline ticket to increase profits or showing the customer two more highly selected products to maximize the likelihood that they will buy more are guided by data-based predictions. Once an organization's staff in knows what the next best action for the company is, they can act on it with little hesitation.

Organizational AI

By this point, you may be wondering why I keep talking about business intelligence in a book about AI. Well, that's because BI is data-driven, and data are critical to many AI applications (at least at the early stages of machine learning, as well as deep learning). Machine learning is made possible by lots of meaningful data plus advanced CPU power. The narrow AI that we have today are trained with data. The more the data we feed it, the more sophisticated the AI becomes. Remember how Alpha GO became so good at what it does? It's because it learns from human data first, and once it surpasses that information, it learns to generate it by playing against itself. Even when we have Strong AI (artificial general intelligence), it will have to learn from data before it can derive higher forms of intelligence.

This whole process should sound quite familiar. After all, it's very similar to how humans develop intelligence. At birth, we make use of the brain (hardware and software) to interpret our environment. We learn by understanding the data we collect through our sensory organs —eyes, ears, tongue, and even our skin and nerves. By trial and error, we learn. By looking at historical data, we learn. By experimenting, we improve and avoid making mistakes. We know fire is hot, so we try not to touch it. We learn that driving against the traffic is a big no-no, both for legal and safety reasons. We learn that we hate spicy foods and love sour candy, or vice versa.

A machine with the right algorithm can do the same. That's why Alpha GO knows which moves it needs to make to avoid losing.

Although the basic concept behind BI and AI is the same and they follow similar patterns – understand, interpret, and make a conclusion based on data – there are important differences between them. The crucial distinction is the algorithm. Normal BI applications use simple business logic and aggregation to consume the data, while smarter machine learning processes use better algorithms to analyze, consume, understand, and turn the data into applicable knowledge all on their own and can suggest the best course of actions on the basis of it.

Individual productivity

We have now recapped how organizations benefited from the industrial productivity boom, data intelligence advancements, and the AI transformation. So, what's next?

Well, organizations consist of individuals, and individuals carry many of the same characteristics as organizations. We, as individual, care about our finances, our health, our social image and status. We strive to grow, and we always want to learn and improve. With so much in common, it should come as no surprise that we, as individuals, can use the same concepts organizations to improve their performance and productivity to improve our own. The same data, analytics, and AI transformations that work for organization can be applied to individual productivity. In fact, it has already happened in many different ways. Think about the cars we purchase. They allow us to extend our "transportation ability." We already expanded when we tamed horses and learned to ride them, but with the transition to motor vehicles in the early 20th century, we extended that ability exponentially. And that smart phone you have in your pocket or that you're using to read this, consider just how much it improved your ability to access information, sped up your communication, and enhanced your productivity.

Now consider how drastically our abilities were improved with the invention of gun powder in China during the late Tang Dynasty of the 9th century. The subsequent invention of the firearm made the gunpowder even more practical. Guns could pierce a knight's armor, which completely shifted the paradigm for combat and militarism. Battle charges across open fields became a thing of the past now that soldiers could only hope to survive if they had cover from the volley of bullets. The rifle evolved into a machine gun. This new weaponry didn't have to be loaded every shot and could shoot thirty or forty rounds before needing to be reloaded. People really wanted cover then! The history of the firearm is a story of how we extended our ability to cause damage and protect ourselves. When you stop to think about it, the transition from stone, to sword, gun powder, guns, machine guns, and finally the powerful weapons of modern warfare is really amazing.

Again, we can see the same extension of abilities with the invention of paper, another technology invented by the Chinese. Papermaking is traditionally linked to Cai Lun, an imperial eunuch official of the Han dynasty (202 BC-AD 220). In 105 AD, Lun introduced a type of paper made of mulberry and other bast fibers along with fishing nets, old rags, and hemp waste, which reduced the cost of paper production.

Now we come to AI. AI is not a single, clear-cut technological development because it's really an umbrella term that covers many things. Or I should say, it covers almost everything that resemble human intelligence – from telling different colors apart, to driving, cooking, and inventing patents. AI ranges from physical automation, robots, pure intelligences, and combinations of all three. In all cases, as a kind of human intelligence exhibited by machines, AI is an artificial means of extending our basic human cognitive abilities. Our level of human intelligence is determined by the decisions we make, the things we choose, and what we act on. 1+1 is a simple intellectual challenge, but we make use of something to solve it. Whether we decide that $1+1 = 2$ or that $1+1 = 0$ depends on how we process the problem based on what we know, how we interpret the question. First, the decision maker, whether it is human or machine, has to understand what the number 1 means and correctly assess that the + symbol means addition. Then, they have to compute the information using some sort of thinking (for human) or algorithm (for machines). From that, they will make a decision and settle on an answer to the question.

Individual Intelligence

Why wouldn't we want the same efficiency that companies get through technology? And, judging from the anthropological evidence, we always want more. As AI becomes cheaper and smarter, the same holds for personal intelligence. We all want to know more about ourselves. We want to better our health, our personal performance, and be the best selves we can be. We are so fond of our cognitive abilities that even when we are not behaving rationally, we tend to think we are always rational and not making "stupid" decisions. And we also believe data are critical to making better long-term life decisions. We have a utopian mindset: if we get the data right, we will be happy all the time and make decision we don't regret. So why can't we have enhanced personal intelligence? Why has no one built personal intelligence devices that we can use to make better decisions?

There are two major reasons why individual intelligence is not yet a household technology. First, there is the current state of technology. It still costs businesses tens of thousands or even millions to build business-level intelligence. That includes the software required to collect data from different parts of the organization, group data that doesn't "talk" to each other together, analyze the data to find out what it's telling us. None of these are easy tasks by any means. The current technology is too still expensive to apply at a personal level. Although data intelligence products have improved a lot over the last ten years, it's still not ready for everyday use, nor is it easy to apply at an individual level. We simply don't have the AI commodity technology to interpret data in such a fine-grained and nuanced way. Before that happens, we need AI technology to become a commodity.   Only when AI becomes a commodity, the technologies will be cheap enough to be accessible by everyone in a developed country – imagine having a cell phone back in the 1990s. Only when AI becomes a commodity, it will level the playing fields for the less resourced – imagine commuting 20 Miles to work without a car vs someone has a car back in the 1910s. Only when AI becomes a commodity, it will become invisible in our lives – we take plastics, grains, and salt for granted- they used to be the new great things.

And then, of course, are the concerns about privacy. Data privacy could be an issue if people hesitate to make their own data easily accessible to machines. Thanks to social media, these concerns have relaxed substantially, with the younger generations already used to sharing everything they do online with little worry about who might be able to access it. But it's important not to become complacent about our data even when we want to benefit from sharing it. We need better regulations to control data use and movement. Without control over our own data, we lose our privacy and can be easily manipulated.

What we also need, however, is an enhancement of individual intelligence, an ability to find out more about ourselves objectively so we can make informed, data-driven decisions. To automate and enhance our personal intelligence, we need to take it one step up further by using artificial individual intelligence.

Individual Decision Automation

As an architect who is highly experienced with analytics and automation, I foresee that the technology will become cheaper and easier for us to apply at the personal level in the very near future. The chasm is big – I don't want to minimize the challenge – but it is very doable. Individual data are more scattered, unstructured, originate from disparate sources, and are much harder to monitor. There is also no enforced or standardized way of collecting this data from the public, so it is far more "free form" than corporate data, which is meticulously compiled and ordered.

Imagine a world in which we could understand ourselves the way those businesses that spend millions on data analysis understand their performance and operations. We could become as efficient as we would like to be. And if we used this to track and analyze financial decisions the way businesses do, how many more of us could avoid bankruptcy, invest smartly, and reach our financial goals? Not having to rely on our gut instincts and fuzzy math skills to tell us whether we can really afford a bigger house or a home theater system could save many of us a lot of trouble down the road.

And if we could use the same processes businesses use to understand their facilities and logistics, what would that mean for our health outcomes? If we could have a clear and objective understanding of our body's intake, heart rate, kidney functions, and other vital signs, how much smarter could we be about our food, fitness, and work habits? We will never be perfect specimens of health because we naturally want to indulge now and then. But we would do far better if we knew when would be an ideal time to relax and have a bowl of ice cream so that it wouldn't send our blood sugar levels completely out of balance. We're not far from this new world. We just need entrepreneurs who have vision and a general public that understands and embraces the possibilities.

Artificial Individual Intelligence

Imagine taking all this a step further. You wouldn't even have to manage all these small tasks yourself. Instead, someone intelligent can make all these small and big decisions for you. It would be like having a personal assistant working for you but with a consultant's ability to make better decisions for you.

Artificial Individual Intelligence is the next phase of personal intelligence advancement. Again, personal intelligence is a concept that parallels business intelligence – it is our ability to know how well we are doing at personal level, in general or compared to others. But like business intelligence, it doesn't make a lot of decisions on our behalf.

Business- or organization-oriented AI takes that even one step further. They use software and hardware engineering to create machines that will actually make decisions on behalf of humans. Alpha GO decides on the next move to win a game of GO and Amazon smart warehouse stores and moves inventory on its own instead of waiting for human input. Artificial individual intelligence will come to us the same way. With software and hardware engineering, we will create machines that take decisions out of our hands and make them on our behalf.

Artificial Individual Intelligence Is Not New

Artificial Individual Intelligence sounds futuristic but it isn't new at all. If you look around, you'll see plenty of these products already on the market. Nest is one example of an artificial individual intelligence product. The Nest Learning Thermostat is an electronic, programmable, and self-learning Wi-Fi-enabled thermostat that optimizes its heating and cooling settings to conserve energy while keeping home and building occupants comfortable. It is based on a machine learning algorithm: for the first weeks, users have to manually regulate the thermostat in order to provide it with a reference data set. The thermostat then learns people's schedule, at which temperature they like the room, and when they make adjustments. Using built-in sensors to track the location of smartphones, it can shift into energy saving mode when it realizes nobody is at home.

Nest can be considered Narrow Artificial Individual Intelligence if we use the term very loosely. First, while it does its task very well, it is still performing only one narrow task. It also uses its machine learning algorithm to learn about the behavior of only a small group of people (those who inhabit the house or building it regulates). So basically, Nest's AI will help you make one decision and make it very well: whether to adjust your thermostat for the perfect ambient temperature and to save on energy. Recall that, in Chapter 1, I called a thermostat a kind of dumb AI. Although Nest can schedule adjustments and automatically modify the temperature settings, I would still call it a dumb AI, although a smarter one to be sure. However, I also know that we've only seen the start of smart thermostats. I expect it will continue to improve and factor in more variables than just the temperature and the user's schedule. Maybe, at some point in the future, Nest will analyze the body temperatures of the humans present in the home so that it will know to turn up the A/C after someone has been working out or turn up the heat when someone is sick and shivering under a blanket.

Of course, there are concerns that even a smart thermometer will be used against our own interests. If the manufacturer decides to enter into partnership with a dairy producer, for instance, it might manipulate the algorithm and turn up the heat slightly to influence individuals to buy more ice cream. Since it is a violation of the individual's interests, this would be a violation of my rules for Artificial Individual Intelligence

Outside-In Artificial Individual Intelligence

When you talk to a virtual assistant today, you may have a conversation like the one that follows.

You: I want to buy AA batteries. What are my options?

VA: Sure/ You can buy a 12 pack of Nile Brand AA Batteries for $11.49/ Do you want to make the purchase?

You: No. What other choices do I have?

VA: There is a 24 pack of Nile Brand AA batteries for $22.49. Do you want to make the purchase?

You: No. What other choices do I have?

VA: I am sorry. That's all that is available to sale at the moment.

Then, you go to the largest retail store's website and find that there are 48 others AA battery brands available for sale. What is happening here? Why were those not presented to you by your AI virtual assistant?

The answer is simple: the current AI were created by business for business. They're meant to encourage you to buy more, spend more, and benefit their stockholders. They only look like they're working for you.

A map-routing AI will show you advertisements you don't want to see, and can route you so you drive near their customers' locations. Ever wonder why your GPS's restaurant locator sometimes misses the smaller establishments? Is it a coincidence?

A retailer's AI will show you only the deals that would maximize their profit. It's clear who their virtual assistant is really assisting.

A real estate AI broker will show you properties that would benefit the company the most, putting your housing needs and budget second in priority.

It's the nature of business to aim at these outcomes, and we can't blame them for using whatever tools they have available. But we don't have to be manipulated by third-party AI, or intelligence of any kind, especially those that know more about us than we do. We can take control and put these technologies back into our own hands.

Power to the People

Most of us welcome new technologies, but we're afraid AI will take our jobs, make us irrelevant, and help corporations manipulate us for their own gains. We want AI on our side because we know that whoever has it will benefit tremendously. If big corporations have all the AI power working for them, they will use it to take advantage of us. And if the AI itself is smarter than us and decides to put its own interests ahead of ours, it could choose to eliminate the whole human race before we can threaten its existence!

We should prepare for that and take the power back before it's used against us. We should create AI that puts humans first and gives power to the people. We equip ourselves with extended intelligence like AI so we can make better decisions, not so we can have others dictate our decision-making. And this brings us back to the main focus of the book, that idea that we should tame AI rather than fight against it.

Taming AI

In the thousands of years of documented history, human beings have always had helpers. We domesticated dogs so they could protect us, hunt with us, and learn to live with us as their masters. We tamed horses so they could be used for transportation and to make agriculture more efficient. Now, we have a chance to tame AI.

Taming AI will, of course, be different than taming dogs and horses. We won't be trying to outsmart AI and make it respect us, and we won't try to convince it that we can work together. We also won't need to lure them into working for us by giving it fuel or energy, the way we used food to entice formerly wild animals. I will go into more details about taming AI in the last part of the book.

Inside-out Artificial Individual Intelligence

With the goal of taming AI in mind, I want to introduce the term Inside-Out AI. This is a concept I am coining to represent a classification of AI technology that is built for the individual. The Inside-Out AI is an AI that thinks on behalf of the individual in order to benefit the individual.

The Inside-Out AI mapping system will not take you to the nearest commercial establishment but to the location you want to go, using the roads that would be most convenient or pleasant for you to travel on. The Inside-Out AI virtual assistant would find you the best deals on the products you need, not the best deals on the brands that a particular company wants you to purchase. And the Inside-Out AI will help you find the home that best suits your preferences while matching your budget, not the homes the realtors are hoping to sell. The Inside-Out AI can also fact check and consult multiple sources of information to make sure that you are making the most informed decision, rather than restricting your information to the ones available on some third-party site.

Counter AI with AI

Developing Inside-Out AI agents is the best way for us to protect against rogue AI and malevolent hackers who can control AI for their own purposes. It might sound like a crazy sci-fi scenario, but we know the technology is going to keep improving. And it is incredibly difficult to make any complex systems perfect. We will not be able to compete with AI when it taps into huge data sources and becomes smarter than us.

The only feasible option is for us to partner with AI. To fight AI with AI. And that's why we need MaaS AI, which are Inside-Out AI. If instead of having "anti-rogue" AI machine built by corporation to police and keep bad AI away, we have millions (us) of AI enabled Human to counter rogue AI together. As in the old sayings that "A single arrow is easily broken, but not ten in a bundle", and "None of us is as smart as all of us".

MaaS Considers AI Our Extension

We need to treat AI as an extension of us, as our extended partner, rather than a competitor. There are two ways we can position AI technologies. The first is to develop strong AI that operate on their own with their own thought patterns and personalities. This is the kind of AI we see in the movies about technology gone rogue, from HAL 9000 in 2001: A Space Odyssey to Skynet in the Terminator franchise. The AI can make decisions that are not regulated and it may use means that are a bit too ruthless to achieve its goals.

The second option is to consider AI as a tool, the same way we treat all our other tools. AI extends human intelligence the same way cars extend our mobility, hammers extend our ability to exert physical power, the same way printer make our writing faster, nicer, and more consistent. AI is not so different than the microphones we use to amplify the volume and range of our voices or the rifles we use to extend the range and severity of damage we could inflict with our bare hands.

These inventions help us learn, evolve, and rule the planet. We want AI to help us continue to do so by amplifying our intelligence.

Seamless Integration and User Experience

For AI to be an extension of our abilities, it has to be useful and easily controllable – and the easier the better.

To be of much use, a car needs to be easily steered and able to comfortably seat a human. A hammer needs to be customized for its particular uses. It's not impossible to use a sledge hammer to drive in a small nail, but it's not the perfect tool for the job. Likewise, you could tear down a wall with a small claw hammer, but it's clearly designed for other uses. In any case, the hammer amplifies and extends our power, but does so even more when it is designed for doing a job with ease. Likewise, for the gun to be of genuine use to us, it needs to have a handle that allows us to hold it comfortably. It also needs safety features to keep us from inadvertently causing damage, which would outweigh its usefulness, especially if careless handling costs us our lives.

It's the same for AI. Within Mind-as-a-Service, our AI extension is called a "Mind-as-a-Service Intelligent Agent" a.k.a. M.I.A. It will only be a genuinely beneficial extension of our intelligence if it fits the following three requirements.

1.   *Have High Intelligence* – For the MaaS AI to fully understand our strengths and weaknesses, and to assist us intelligently, the AI must have superior intelligence to be useful. We definitely don't want an AI dumber than us. It needs, then, to be integrated and equipped with basic technology. Chapter 7 will cover the intelligence DNA of a MaaS Inside-Out AI agent in greater detail.

2.   *Understand Limitations* –There are many words that we use to denote human limits: conscience, ethics, good judgment. In managing technology, it can be called risks management, fail-safe, regulation, lawful activities, and governance. AI needs to be able to understand and comply with these limitations.

Chapter 8 will cover the preference, personality, ethical capabilities of the MaaS Inside-Out AI agent.

3. *Understand real human decision-making factors* – We make decisions based on our needs and wants. When I am happy, for example, I have different food preferences than when I am upset. In Chapter 9, we will go over the emotional connectivity between humans and AI and how it is critical to ensuring that it fully understands us and our needs.

The Second Brain for Extra Productivity

Once we have seamless or near-seamless integration with our AI, the MaaS AI can make decisions and act on our behalf with minimized manual intervention. The MaaS MIA will consider all options and come to the conclusion that will suit us the most. This artificial brain will spend its energy thinking, freeing our own brains to engage in more cognitive and creative tasks or simply giving it some much needed rest. It will connect directly with our brains and provide intelligence that we could never have physically processed on our own. The second brain will become part of us and help us navigate the new AI-driven world.

Whether the world adopts Mind as a Service or not, MaaS AI will give MaaS adopters an edge over those who don't have AI on their side.

The MIA Can Learn and Grow Effortlessly

Have you seen the movie The Matrix? In it, Keanu Reeves's character Neo acquires new skills by "downloading" them from a program. He then says, "I know Kung Fu."

The MIA can do the same, so long as the new skill or knowledge is organized in a format that it can consume. The skills could be purchased, if needed, and "downloaded" to the MIA. It could be a rental scheme, in which your MIA can rent a "skill" or set of information and then release it after a given amount of time.

Personalized Skills

There is no reason to worry that we will be limiting our knowledge with the same canned versions of knowledge and skills available to the MIA. Remember, the MIA is an extension of the human, and it is personified with the personality, preference, and ethics of its user. The person can actually learn the skill acquired by their MIA by getting the MIA to train and teach them.

Consider the way we drive, for instance. It's our personalities that dictate whether we prefer a smooth ride with minimal turns or the winding scenic route with minimal traffic. It's also our personalities that dictate whether we prefer arriving to our destination as soon as possible or prefer having a more pleasant riding experience.

Everything depends on the person. The good, the bad, the ugly – AI amplifies what is already part of us. In Chapter 12, we will discuss the governance and regulations that are needed to ensure that this amplification doesn't lead us to dark and dangerous consequences.

Decision Outsourcing

With an AI (the MIA) that knows everything about you, right down to your preferences, but also has more intellectual power, you can outsource your decisions. Remember Mark from the beginning of the chapter? Instead of trying to put together a humdrum party in a constant state of panic, he decided to outsource all the planning decisions for his girlfriend's birthday party. The result? A perfect setting and all the mundane and dull tasks, like looking at seemingly endless ring options, done for him. There are thousands of potential solutions to his non-life-threatening but still important problem. He wants to have only the viable options presented to him, the ones that meet certain basic criteria. Once his options have been narrowed down, it's up to him to make the final decision!

American adults make thousands of decisions on a daily basis, starting from whether you should wake up now or hit the snooze button, what to eat, when to leave for work, and what to bring up when you're having an important conversation.

Decision outsourcing is one of the ways MaaS helps us be more productive. There are, after all, two ways we can become more productive. First, as we discussed above, we can add intelligence capabilities. But we can also simply free up our limited brain power so that it is focused only on the most significant problems. The way to do this is to only make high value decisions and leave the easy ones to our AI assistants. Outsourcing your decisions the way Mark did is precisely how we can achieve that.

There are many decisions that require superhuman intelligence, like winning against a GO champion. And while it's those "sexier" uses of AI that get all the attention, AI can also help us deal with the sub-human decisions as well. Calling a cab, finding the easiest way from point A to point B, finding the cheapest train or plane ticket to our destination, deciding what to eat after eating oriental food for five meals in a row — none of these decisions require much intelligence. But it does require intelligence that understand you as a person — your preferences, your moods, your emotions. An MIA will have that ability. It will not only know facts and data; it will know you as a person.

The nth Brain

The MIA is a MaaS AI, which is a combination of software and hardware engineering. Its processing power can be scaled the same way we scale all other software and hardware. We can add hardware "brain power" or even cloud processing power as needed.

Imagine that your MIA "lives" in an environment like Amazon Web Services or Microsoft Azure. You could add processing power any time you wanted it. Say you're going on a date and you need to be at 3,000% intelligence capacity with real-time, lightning-fast response times. You would simply tap into cloud processing and boost up your power for, say, five hours. In other words, you will literally be renting brain power!

MaaS Orchestrates AIs and Performs Real-Time Integration

The MIA agent is more than an interface that integrates seamlessly with human beings at an ethical, intellectual, and emotional level. The MIA agent also coordinate and automatically looks for new functions, and make the decision to acquire new skills for us.

MIA agents can acquire new decision skills on our behalf when it is needed. For example, if the user wants to know how she can spend her Saturday afternoon, the MIA agent can automatically connect with external AI services, such as event services and restaurant services, and coordinate all the available options. The MIA can then make a decision based on the availability, budget, preferences, and mood of the human and select the best plan accordingly.

The Superpower Buffet

Your MIA is a jack of all trades. You don't need your AI to do everything, to know everything, or to be able to make the best decisions. You only need it to do what a great leader does: know where to go and who to talk to.

Imagine yourself as a superhero: AI MAN. Your superpower is to summon different types of intelligence capabilities at will. If you have to cook Thai food for 20 people, you seamless acquire the knowledge of a Thai chef via your MIA. In two days, you can acquire the mind of a professional home stager so you can arrange your living room to impress your guests. That's just one example off the top of my head – I'm in party planning mode as I write this – but the sky is the limit!

The Invisible New World

The concept of extending human capabilities through AI may sound strange to some readers. You might be imagining people walking around with all sorts of weird devices attached to them, looking like movie cyborgs or Robocop. This is not at all what I have in mind. The world may actually become quieter, not full of hulking half-robots, because people will be smarter and calmer thanks to the security and knowledge brought about by AI. They will have better answers and smarter comments because they will be constantly advised by their MaaS. And of course, getting help from an MIA is optional. Like today, you can always choose to live "off the grid."

Like all new technologies, the integration may be cumbersome at first and require constant interaction with the AI agent, telling it things like:

"No, I don't want that."

"I meant this, not that."

"I have a special preference for my mom."

"I don't like her. Please ignore her for me."

But things will get better. AI is smart and self-improving. Plus, we will have upgrades that better organize its ethics, preferences, and decision history.

Just think back to the first video game system you ever tried. If it was in the 1980s, you had a controller with a few simple buttons. That limited the ways you could interact with the video games. All of your in-game options were limited to what the combination of four directional arrows and the A, B, Start, and Select buttons could allow. Soon, video game systems hit the shelves with bulkier controllers with more and more buttons. The video games got more complicated and once we mastered all of the controller's functions, we could interact with the game far more smoothly. And then boom! The Nintendo Wii came out and completely changed the controller game with its Wii Remote. It was smaller, and had about as many buttons as were on the 1980s controllers, but it had a motion sensor that allowed your hand motions to guide the action on the screen. And four years later in 2010, Microsoft rolled out the Kinect, a line of motion sensing input devices for their Xbox 360 and Xbox One video game consoles, as well as Windows PCs. Using a webcam-style add-on peripheral, it enabled users to control and interact with their console or computer without a needing a controller. The device could pick up the player's gestures and spoken commands, creating a seamless gaming experience where moving your body creates corresponding movements in the game. But that wasn't the apex of gaming integration. Six years later, Sony Interactive Entertainment launched its PlayStation VR, a virtual realty headset, which places the user right inside the game's universe.

The same transformation will happen with AI integration. We're still at the early stages, but once it is complete, we will be fully evolved into a Human x AI model that makes us smarter, better informed, and better protected against the sinister uses of technology.

Human-AI Evolution

Within the next 30 years – or even earlier –many of us will be completely integrated with our MIAs and use them for routine, everyday tasks. We already hear people saying they can't function without their smartphones. Losing the extended ability has a way of making us feel sluggish, weak, and ineffective. Likewise, we won't be able to function fully without our MIA. That's why I call it an AI Evolution. It will no longer simply be that productivity has improved, or that our minds and behavior have been enhanced through better intelligence. Rather, AI will be part of us.

It is a true Human-AI evolution and not an AI takeover because Mind as a Service promotes a human-centric approach to AI that focuses on the individual, unlike most of the current

AI which is programmed to advance corporate and government agendas. We will be skipping ahead in the natural course of evolution by millions of years and artificially evolve into a higher form of intelligence.

If you're ready to look even further than this Human-AI evolution, you're ready for the next chapter. In it, I discuss the next progression of Mind as a Service, which goes beyond the personal MIA and explores the possibility of integrating with other people's AI Minds to achieving far greater things.

CHAPTER 5
BE THE CEO OF YOURSELF: OTHERS' MINDS AT YOUR SERVICE

Talent wins games, but teamwork and intelligence win championships. -Michael Jordan

---

Katie is trying hard not to smirk. She wants to avoid triggering any emotional AI that others might be using. But she is happy. In fact, Katie has never been so confident in her life. She's feeling like she's on top of the world and nothing is impossible. Today is day 68 of the survival game, but it's a whole different game than it was in the first 20 days.

Katie is just an average-looking orphan girl. Her parents died in an accident when she was young. Unfortunately, that set her life on the wrong course. She didn't have the opportunity to attend college or learn many valuable skills. She's hungry and she wants more out of life than the constant struggle. When she heard about his survival game, it felt like the right opportunity finally arrived. She was going to win this and really make something of herself. So, she took out a loan from the bank and hired three AI agents, one from a Fortune 500 business leader, another from a psychologist, and the last one from a doctor.

There was a bit of a rocky start. Katie had no ideas how to use the AI, and the AI hadn't interacted with Katie enough. It also took a lot of time for the AI to learn how Katie behaved socially – her life was so different than those of the AI's owners. In the game, social intelligence matters. Without being able to get much help from her rented AI, Katie navigated the game pretty much on her own in the first 15 days. That meant she made enemies, said the wrong things, and lost an important race for her team. Over just two weeks she had been on the edge of being eliminated seven times, and no one wanted to partner with her. Susan thought she was just a dumb blonde. David thought she wasn't sharp enough and would just be a burden. The other team members teased her and she couldn't bring herself to speak up in her defense or stand her ground. But things took an interesting turn on day 15. Katie's temporary MIA (a collection of high-end rental AI modules) started to kick in and provide intelligence for Katie. One of the rental AI agents – the copy of the psychologist's MIA – began talking to her and delivering constant encouragement to be strong and proactive. Having analyzed her personality traits and recent events, it now advised her on how to use her introverted personality to her advantage. It told her what things to say – and, importantly, how to say them –and what people actually meant when they said something. It taught her to read between the lines and interpret subtle body language, and before long, Katie started to understand the complex dynamics of the group.

The AI agent rented from the business strategist acted as Katie's brain. It analyzed the game for her, and even performed a daily SWOT (Strength, Weakness, Opportunity, Threat) analysis so Katie would know exactly what to aim for every day. During races, the AI would process the game's rules and suggest tactics to win.

The doctor's MIA literally was a life saver for Katie. It's how Katie became a trusted partner to her teammates. With medical knowledge at her fingertips, Katie could provide a lot of help to her teammates and add real value to the team. Staying safe, healthy, and alert isn't easy on a deserted island, but the wealth of wisdom from the doctor's MIA helped her pull through even in those harsh conditions.

Katie knew how to lay low and fly under the radar. But that, on its own, wouldn't have been enough to make it through the game. By seamlessly integrating the rented AIs with her own MIA, she was able to tap on the expertise she needed to gain influence, win races, and make it through situations that would have otherwise been too challenging. After being on the verge of elimination for the first two weeks, she managed to survive another 40 days.

She became confident in her ability to win the game. With just one more days and five finalists left, she would soon find out whether that confidence was warranted. She knows she's the underdog – no one thinks she has a chance at winning – but no one dislikes her enough to vote her out. She had lost everything. And now her dream was finally close to coming true.

In this chapter, you will learn about the second stage in Mind as a Service's evolution:

• Groups of seamlessly connected AI achieving more than one could on its own

• Orchestrating AIs acting as coach and trainer to the others

• Managing AIs becomes a critical skill in this stage of the AI evolution

• AI training skills are an important differentiator in the world of connected AI

• Your own MIA is empowered by third party MIAs

Sun Wukong, the Monkey King

The 16th century classic Chinese novel Journey to the West tells the tale of its protagonist, a monkey named Sun Wukong who is born from a stone and acquires supernatural powers through Taoist practices. After rebelling against heaven and being imprisoned under a mountain by the Buddha, he accompanies the monk Xuanzang on a journey to retrieve Buddhist sutras from "the West." Sun Wukong possesses immense strength – he is able to lift his 13,500 jīn (17,550 lbs) staff with ease. He is also extremely fast, able to travel 108,000 li (13,468 miles) with a single somersault. One of his more unusual superpowers is the possession of magical hair. Each of his hairs possesses magical properties, and they can be transformed into weapons, animals, and even clones of the Monkey King himself. Alone, he already possesses supernatural powers, magic, and skilled fighting abilities. But by creating an army of clones out of his air, he multiplies his strength and can defeat even his most imposing enemies.

When MaaS matures, you'll be able to do the same as Sun Wukong via your MIA(Mind-as-a-Service Intelligent Agent). I can't promise that the future will allow you to morph your hair into clones, but it will allow you to basically clone yourself intellectually, able to perform separate cognitive tasks at once. And all the intellectual clones of yours will work together with the same goals. It will be like multitasking but far more potent and without diminishing the quality of each task.

School of Fishes

You can visualize your intellectual MIAs as a shoal of fish, moving together but each navigating on its own. Fish in a shoal tend to coordinate very well and move in the same directions. These fish schools band together to protect themselves against enemies, knowing that there is strength in numbers. They're like a bundle of sticks that can withstand forces that would snap any individual branch. Predators have to think twice before moving in on a shoal. Trying to snatch one fish will make thousands of them mad and retaliate.

As discussed in Chapter 4, you are outsourcing your decisions to yourself. This allows you to amplify your productivity and intelligence. Essentially, you're building a team with yourself.

Imagine a room with ten people who are all versions of you. Each of them know exactly what you are thinking, and you can brainstorm with ten times the brainpower – literally – to achieve the same goals.

Starling Murmurations

Having a bunch of more intelligent versions you won't simply mean you can get more done in less time. It may also mean you will be able to do things that you can't even imagine now.

Have you even seen pictures of a starling murmuration? That's when hundreds or sometimes thousands of those small birds flock together in a synchronized pattern. I have only seen it once with my own eyes, and it was completely mesmerizing. Each starling taking flight is beautiful and captivating in its own way, but a thousand of them flying together creates the kind of wonder you could never get from something far more wonderful.

Without doing it on purpose, the starlings create natural art that is so beautiful and majestic that no single startling could create it on its own. Even if a starling could get much bigger and much faster, it would still just be a single bird taking flight into the sky. And it doesn't matter how beautiful its plumage, it will still just be an impressive bird soaring. There is nothing, in other words, that you can change in a single starling that will produce the mesmerizing patterns that they can create as a group. And that's precisely my point. There are things you can't simply scale to create. There are abilities we can't begin to imagine before we actually see them. I don't know what a team of you could create when you are all working together – you and, consequently, a team of you are unique after all. But whatever it is, it's sure to be greater than I could imagine.

The sky is really the limit. Just think: how amazing would a bunch of YOUs be?

The collaborative process would be incredibly smooth and efficient. You would never have to waste time trying to convince the other versions of you that your idea is a good one. No need for elaborate drawings, technical white papers, or slideshows to make your case. No 9am conference calls where you try to appease stakeholders and answer to all of their concerns. You – all of you – would already know the details and be on board. How great would that be?

You could have ten, fifty, or even a hundred versions of yourself working simultaneously on a big problem, each handling different tasks but without any friction, all aiming at the same goal. It would be one beautiful, unified team doing what it does best, like a murmuration of starlings in full flight.

Your Personal Think Tank – Others' Minds at Your Service

If you can have a team made up of different versions of you, why not put together a team made up of versions of different people as well?

That development is where we come to the second stage of

the Mind as a Service Evolution: Others' minds at your services.

Imagine yourself in your favorite place (your backyard, by the living room fireplace, inside a corporate war room, on a beach, in your basement...) collaborating with ten people. But this time, they're not all versions of yourself. Five of them are – they're your MIAs – but the others are versions of other people. One MIA is a lawyer's, another is owned by a military general, one has worked closely with a management consultant, one famously defeated all comers in GO, and the other has been learning and adapting with a historian. You've assembled this team of MIAs with one goal: create a five-year strategic plan to expand your two-person t-shirt selling business in Bangkok's tourist area. You want a plan that is stealthy yet aggressive, and that takes into consideration all of your competitors who are selling apparel in the same area. You want to monopolize this street and be the only t-shirt seller, but you want to do it without making enemies in the process.

You know that you could never achieve this on your own. So you're tapping on the strategical mind of the military tactician and the big-picture thinking of the GO champion. You have the vision but you don't have all the answers. No matter how intelligent you become, how many of you there are, or how fast you can think, you are still just you. You are limited – we all are.

You simply don't know what you don't know.

This is where the new evolution of MaaS comes in. You can make up for those deficiencies by tapping the minds of others. You don't care if all ten MIA work together, split up into pairs to work on individual sub-problems, or if the team of five specialists acts as a kind of expert panel that will review every suggestion you put toward them. In fact, all of these MIA are smart enough to figure it out and make these kinds of decisions without you.

Who knows what they will actually do. Who knows what

incredible plans they could come up with. Remember the starlings? We would have no idea how beautiful simple, synchronized flocking could be if we simply contemplated each bird in isolation of the others. The potential of a group of highly skilled people who are seamlessly connected is simply unimaginable.

And I am not even going to try! I'm leaving it up to your imagination. And if you have a more creative way of drawing this picture, let me know!

The Orchestra Conductor

If you go see an orchestra perform, you'll notice that the musicians spend a lot of time looking at the conductor. That's because it's the conductor who is directing the performance. Their primary duties are to give cues to the players that set the tempo, ensure correct entries by members of the ensemble, and "shape" the phrasing where appropriate.

Your collection of MIAs is like an orchestra, and your primary MIA is its conductor. It will help you guide and organize tens, hundreds, or even thousands of third-party MIAs. And it will do more than direct their activities; it will also plan and design how big or small the collection of MIAs should be, how many should be assigned to a given task, and what kind of skills or expertise each will require.

Imagine a big orchestra hall full of people working for you. Now, multiply that by 100. It would be intimidating to lead such a huge team, but your primary MIA will be up to the task. It will be a skilled conductor, and every player will patiently await its instruction.

Do a Lot More, with More

Current automation technologies or consulting firms are always sold with the promise that they'll let you "do more with less." What that means, basically, is that you can automate your tasks and have then done by intelligent machines. You'll get more done with less input, effort, and expense.

But what about doing more with more? If we can do more with less, imagine how much we can do with more. The future won't be a world of "do more with less," but a world of "do more, with less; then do a lot more, with more."

What does that mean? I think you could figure it out yourself, but I'll spell it out anyway. Essentially, it means:

"Do more [with AI automation], with less [manual work and thinking]; then do a lot more [with more AI automation], with more [of YOU]."

"So, Brian are you saying that I won't need to work anymore?" you may be asking. "Doesn't that literally mean AI will take my job? Or, really, that I'm taking my own job?" Well, not really. It's true that you will be outsourcing some of your work to AI. But remember that your MIA ¬(or whatever AI team that your MIA creates) is configured to your personality, preference, and a set of ethical constraints. They are going to make decisions and present you with the best options, but you will be ultimately responsible for happens next. Whether you do great things or bad things with your MIA will all be up to you. All it can do is make simple, everyday decisions on your behalf, like what you should eat, when you should leave to catch a meeting on time, and whether a job offer will be a good fit for you. But the major decisions will still be yours – and even if we do ever come to delegate those, it won't be for a long time. Think of the auto-pilot function on any airplane. Planes can basically fly themselves from one city to another, across the ocean in any weather. But we still need human judgement and experience to make sure there is a safe take-off and landing. The stakes are too high to allow AI to make all our decisions for us. And that is acknowledged by all the aviation governance organizations, like the Federal Aviation Administration(FAA) in the United States, or Transport Canada in Canada. To make sure that we retain the control we need and protect ourselves and our future, we will also require regulations and governance (this will be dealt with in greater depth in Chapter 12).

You Are the CEO of "You Enterprise"

Let's take a step further. Imagine again those ten people in favorite location, but this time they are all the senior executives of your Fortune 500 company. This team's roster includes your Chief Resources Officer, Chief Financial Officer, Chief Technology Officer, Chief Negotiator, your business strategist, and one is even your life coach. Your job every day is to listen to all of the great suggestions coming from this think tank – with that kind of brilliance assembled in one place, it would be irresponsible not to. At first, you might question everything or dislike all of their suggestions. But as time goes by, they'll get smarter and smarter, start to understand you better, and become far less generic.

This kind of team will be available to you. They'll be hired out from professionals who have supplied them with their specialized knowledge and experience. Each of these team members are professionals and may have a real job somewhere that allows them to grow and learn day by day. The more the owners of each of these MIAs learn, the more you benefit. And, of course, those owners benefit, too, from leasing these MIAs to others like you.

Every MaaS AI Is as Unique as You Are

Every AI on the market is somewhat generic. They are built in a certain way to achieve some defined purpose and they are identical to other AIs in the same line. So, what do I mean by insisting that each AI will be unique?. This is one of the ways that MaaS will be different than the AI built by corporations. It's also a feature that will give humans an edge in the clash with AI.

In Chapter 1, I introduced Mind as a Service as a human-first framework that considers AI an extension of the human. In other words, as a tool to amplify human intelligence.

The MaaS Intelligent Agent (MIA) integrates with human users at the levels of intellect, personality, and emotions. They are, in other words, personified by the owner. Unless there is some other person out there with the exact same personality, emotional profile, and level of intelligence as you, no two MIAs will be identical.

In Chapter 4, saw how the MIA can learn, grow, and become resourceful. The MIA will have ability to make decisions on your behalf if you delegate some authority to it, or make recommendations with options that closely match your preferences.

In this Chapter, we're seeing how the MIA's personality can be amplified even further with additional help from other MIAs. Because it amplifies what is, at base, a unique personality profile, each MIA, regardless of the number of sub-MIAs it is composed of, is itself unique.

Road Rage and Model Drivers

The way cars behave on the road can serve as a mechanical analogy for this uniqueness. When we drive a car off the dealership lot, we're behind the wheel of the same car that hundreds of other drivers use. The car extends our mobility by making it easier for us to travel from point A to point B. But the car can be driven in many different ways to accomplish that. You could follow all the traffic laws to a T and obey every traffic signs, opting for the slowest and safety lanes. You could be a more leisurely driver, fond of taking the long way if it means there is better scenery and with an unfortunate tendency to become distracted behind the wheel. Or you can tailgate the other cars, cut through lanes just to gain a few extra feet of distance, and slide through all the stop signs while driving well above the posted speed limit – as long as you don't see a police car anywhere.

We don't consider the car as different cars, but they still inherit the attributes of their drivers. The same applies to MIAs. They start off more or less identical when they come out of the box, so to speak. But soon, each MIA becomes acquainted with its owner and will inherit their behavior and characteristics. Of course, cars only display our behavior when we turn the wheel or press down on the pedal. Once we step out of the driver's seat, the car ceases to be prudent, reckless, or anything other than a generic vehicle. Th MIA, however, stores the behavior and the traits in its memory. It won't be wiped clean when we stop actively using it, but will continue to work on our behalf with all of our preferences and dispositions.

The Real-Life Pokémon Trainer

Thanks to the popular Pokémon Go app, most people are now familiar with the popular franchise of card games, television shows, and video games. Pokémon (short for "pocket monsters") are wild creatures that are captured, tamed, and raised by Pokémon trainers, who then send them to battle with other Pokémon for sport. The trainer's work is critical. Each Pokémon of a given species has the same characteristics in the wild. But under the trainer's care, they develop particular skills, powers, and even evolve into different subspecies (the well-known Pikachu, for instance, will evolve into the lesser known Pichu and Raichu). Winning Pokémon battles and tournaments, then, requires more than just collecting the individual Pokémon; it also requires dedicated training and upbringing.

The Pokémon, further, can learn to work together, orchestrated by the trainer. Two trainers with the same type of Pokémon can have widely diverging performances based on their ability to help their creatures cooperate.

The Pokémon are just like your car: it's the same as everyone else's when you acquire it, but it becomes unique with the trainer's input. The difference is that the Pokémon learns, grows, and gets better at what they do. In this way, they are similar to a MaaS AI: they develop a personality and skill-set under the guidance of the trainer, but don't need the trainer to be actively present and controlling every action for that personality to continue having an effect. Likewise, you, as the owner of the MIA, will train, grow, and invest into it so that it adapts to your character and abilities. Your MIA, for example, won't come to you with accounting skills. But if you determine that those skills will be useful and cost effective in the long-term, you can invest in an accounting MIA module. Note, however, that while the module will perform basic accounting tasks for you, it's still up to your own skill and judgment how to use the MIA's accounting abilities. Whether it's to manage your personal finances so you can save for retirement or whether it's to maximize the amount of money you can put into your gambling habit will be up to your input.

Skills Still Matter, But Different Skillsets

Many people fear that the coming of AI will mean the loss

of our value as individuals. You probably know by now that I disagree with that. Our skills will still have value, but they'll be different types of skills than the ones we find useful now. It is the skills involved in controlling, maintaining, and investing in multiple AI to work in concert that will be especially prized. It's just like cooking: everyone can buy the same ingredients but what matters is how inspired our combinations are and how good we are with a frying pan or wire whisk. We all know experienced cooks who can take a recipe and make it into something that smells, looks, and tastes amazing. And, then again, we also know people who can follow a recipe to the letter only to end up wondering what went wrong when the dish comes out barely edible.

The MIAs are like the chef's ingredients. We're still many, many years away from an Artificial General Intelligence. But we will soon see a transition from narrow AI to strong AI. And that transition will involve skillful management on our part.

The New Superhero: AI Man

Your MIA is a jack of all trades. But you won't need an AI that can do everything, know everything, and make all the best decisions. Really, what you'll need your personal AI to do what all the best leaders do: know where to go and who to talk to.

Picture our superhero again: AI Man. Your special power is the ability to summon any intellectual ability or knowledge in a split second. You can solve puzzles as fast as you want, tell who is who right away, remember every single detail of your life in the most fine-grained way. You can also multitask and solve multiple hard problems at once. And every April you discover to your relief that you can prepare your taxes with no effort. Whether you're going to your little sister's wedding or filing for divorce from your spouse, you'll be able to summon your super powers.

With MIAs, we can all become AI Man. Let's say your sister's wedding is on July 30, 2025. You let the MIA know the date, time, and location. Your MIA the goes to work. And that's good news because you're not much of a planner. Your MIA, thankfully, knows that about you and has already taken steps to learn planning and personal organization skills. It will expertly map out the logistics and tell you everything you need to do to make sure you get there on time. Your MIA will interact with a travel agent's MIA, who is known to have great care of her customers. With that connection, the travel MIA will get to work booking a flight and finding suitable accommodations.

Your MIA will even go a step further than your usual well-organized wedding guest. It will then connect to the wedding planner's MIA to learn about the theme, event details, and venue. It will also enlist your sister's personal MIA to help pick out a gift that she will cherish. Lastly, your MIA will make sure you will have enough energy and time to attend the wedding. It knows you place a high priority on attending this event, so it is will clear up your schedule, send cancelation notices, and make sure you get enough sleep.

Pay-as-You-Think Intelligence

That sounds great is, doesn't it? But how can someone have that much intelligence at their disposal? And even if it was possible, where would they find all the money to pay for it? Maybe if you were Tony Stark, the fictional tycoon behind Marvel's Iron Man, you'd have the resources you need. All abilities, productivities, and external means of intelligence cost money. Unless, of course, you happen to be a real-life superhero who acquired their powers through a radioactive spider bite or were blessed by ancient alien super power. While I won't discount those possibilities, I'd say that in 99.999% of the cases, you won't be fortunate enough to acquire any skills or power through those means.

So, without X-Men-style mutations and radioactive experiments imparting these abilities, who is supplying these cognitive superpowers?

Well, in every area of human life, we rely on experts. If you need helps moving, you hire a mover. If you need world-class food, you hire a chef to source the ingredient and cook them for you. If you're looking for a fine dining experience, you hire a server through a restaurant to make sure every part of your meal is taken care of. And if you need help with your finances, you hire an accountant who can take a look at your situation and factor in your goals and needs.

It will be the same in the world of AI evolution. Things will still cost money. Convenience will still cost money. Professionalism will still cost money. And, yes, winning will still cost money.

So, an AI that is trained by a master creative director to design the best visuals will cost money. An AI that is trained by an experienced lawyer will be able to win court cases against an inexperienced lawyer with a low-quality AI with shallow training. You will hire that lawyer's AI the same way you would hire any lawyer today – with costs to match.

Gotta Pay the Bill

Let's take a second to immerse ourselves in the MaaS future. Each of us has an intelligent agent (MIA) that we train, upgrade, and integrate with. When we learn a new skills or experience something new, they become more valuable as well they acquire the corresponding skills and improved intelligence. And when that isn't enough and we need additional help, we buy or rent AI modules to improve our MIA. If we need to build a think tank, we hire specialists and experts. Or if we're dedicated enough, we spend years studying for a new profession and become a hirable expert ourselves.

Basically, there will be no dramatic changes in the way things work. If we need expert help, we'll have the same two options (albeit in enhanced forms) that we have today:

1.   *Study and learn the skills*. Or, we can pay money to acquire the skills with our MIA, but it will require an investment in time and money.

2.   *Hire a professional*. Instead of hiring a real person, we

will have the option of hiring their MIA and still get to benefit from real expertise and critical skills.

Expert advice is never cheap, and an expert's MIA is no exception. Where do you make money? Most of us have a job that helps us pay the bills. But in the world of MaaS, you'll be able to do more. There will be an entire economy built around our AI agents. You will upgrade and personalize your MIA so that it acquires some very specific set of skills. The result might be an MIA that has the skills to be a lighting expert, an architect, or a meditation coach. So why not lease out your MIA to serve others and pocket the reward?

In this chapter, we saw how we can draw on third-party MIAs to enrich our own. The following chapter will explore the other side of that coin: how you and your MIA will be providing services to others, and how this will give rise to a new employment or business class. I will also discuss an innovative concept called BYOAI™, which stands for Bring-Your-Own-Artificial-Intelligence™. BYOAI™, in a nutshell, means that you will no longer be hired as an individual, but will instead be hired as an individual in combination with your MIA. As we will see, this has the potential to earn you a higher pay, but it will also mean you are competing with people based on their AI management skills.

CHAPTER 6

THE NEW EMPLOYMENT MODEL: YOUR MIND PROVIDING SERVICES TO OTHERS

Invest in yourself now and reap the dividends day after day after month after year." -Jack LaLanne

---

In this chapter, you will learn about:

• How "Human + AI" will be the new Mind-as-a-Service employment model
• Why humans are not doomed to become to "useless class"
• Why humans love to work with humans
• The Mind-as-a-Service Social Class
• BYOAI – Bring Your Own Artificial Intelligence
• New Mind-as-a-Service business models
• The new job categories for the MaaS age
• The new currency of power in an AI-driven world

In Chapter 4, we saw how seamlessly integrating our minds with AI will allow to access extra help and exponentially improve our productivity. In Chapter 5, we took it one step further by looking at how we can further improve our lives and multiply our productivity by accessing other people's AIs. In this chapter, we will turn the table and discuss how you can send your Intelligent Agent MIA to work for other people on your behalf. This will be the new employment class. Technically speaking, you will be a service provider in one form of employment, while also being a contractor who can use different instantiations of your MIA to take on multiple jobs for different customers.

One service provider handling many tasks

Imagine, you own a consulting firm like Accenture or Infosys. You need to hire people to handle all of your projects because you have so many clients and you need different types of professionals to do specialized work. You'll need, for instance, an accountant to handle accounting and tax reporting for you. You'll also have to hire consultants who you can send out to help your customers with various projects. You'll need HR people to manage your internal hiring operation.

Normally, you'd need an impressive team to get all of this done. But in the world of MaaS, you can do everything yourself by using the right AI modules! Don't know accounting? Even if you're hopeless in math, you can train your MIA to balance your books. Your MIA can also be your intro operation person to manage your benefits. You can be your own consultant and then send an AI version out virtually to all your customers. You might even hire a senior Mind-as-a-Service trainer to lead 20 MIAs. You will have a virtual team of professionals, with a large, human-backed think tank behind each of them. Instead of spending 8 hours working for you, the humans behind these MIAs might only need to check in for an hour per week to make sure the AI is performing as well as they would.

Hire one to do a lot, and much faster

If you're running a simpler operation, you might not need an AI team at your beck and call. You could do just fine with one MIA that is equipped with many skills. That way, you could work as, say, a salesperson in retail furniture. While you're helping customers find the best furniture options, you can put your AI to work looking for better matches. Your AI could also locate the best shipping deal for your customers.

Things will be faster, more efficient, and far more convenient.

Humans: the useless class?

Many people are concerned that humans will become obsolete, essentially becoming the useless human class once they have no way to keep up with the efficiency of AI. Even if you can hire someone to mobilize, manage, and coordinate multiple AI modules, why not simply take the human out of the equation? If an AI could do a better job of this than a human, why not replace them? The result: humans become obsolete and are served by independent machines without human oversight or intervention.

I disagree with that narrative. I don't believe humans will devolve into a useless class. Rather, I believe that we will evolve into a class that is superior to that of humans on their own. The human class will become Human + AI. A useless human class (an AI - Human class if you will) means that humans don't add any value to the work being done. But how crazy is that? After all, we didn't come to rule the earth because we could walk; we rule it because we can work together and create great things.

As you can imagine, there are different opinions about this. One theory, proposed by the historian Yuval Noah Harari, considers human being — along with every other organism on the planet – an algorithm. Unlike an algorithm coded by a programmer, this one is built over millions of years of evolutions, through incremental improvements and adaptations of the mind. One of the outcomes of this is that, since any algorithm can be replaced by another one, no matter how they were created or executed, then the human algorithm could be replaced by AI. Under this theory, our algorithm is nothing special. While it's built out of our brain, body, and nerves, it's fundamentally a decision-making procedure based on complicated processes that are logical, emotional, and instinctive. But in the end, all decisions – whether they are wise or not – are based on something. And it is that something, that basis for our decision-making, that an artificial algorithm can latch on to and essentially replace us. Current technology may not be advanced enough to build algorithms as sophisticated as the human mind, but when it does, there is no reason why these algorithms shouldn't replace humans and perform all of the same functions we do – only better and faster.

I won't argue with the theory on the point that, theoretically, the human brain's capabilities could be replaced by something artificial. But if, and only if, they have all the same functions as a human, of course. And that's what complicates the picture drawn by this theory. Take the example again of cars. We made them to make our movement more efficient. We can replace most of our motor capabilities with cars, using our legs mostly to move around stores, sidewalks, restaurants, and inside our homes, but rarely to travel any significant distance. No one would argue that we won't be able to replace that remaining mobility with technology. We can already move around these spaces by using machines such as scooters, moving stairs, or elevators. So, why don't we just outsource all of our mobility to machines? It would surely be more efficient to simply be carried from our bed to our workplace, and then to our desks, all without lifting a finger. The reason we don't do it is simple: it's not worth it. Cost and convenience certainly play a role. Cars have become widespread because they provide genuine value for the investment we place in them. Replacing all of our mobility with vehicles, however, is just too cost ineffective. We may – and only may, since nothing about this is certain –eventually develop some advanced technology that will help us travel short distances, browse, and stroll without the use of our legs and more efficiently than our legs could. But until we develop that technology and make it cheap as well, we will be, at best, in a transition period.

It's the same with intelligence. In theory, we can replace human intelligence with an algorithm. But doing so won't be easy and it won't be cheap. While we await the perfection and affordability of these technologies, Mind-as-a-Service will be in place to minimize the initial clash and help with the transition.

Human are social animals

The cost of the technology is just one consideration. Another important one is that we, as humans, are social animals. Most of us like being around, and don't get the same social fulfilment from machines. That alone is a strong obstacle to humans being replaced by machines or artificial intelligence.

We are wired to be with others and to need, desire, and crave relationships of various kinds. Adam Wyatz, Associate Professor of Management and Operations at the Kellogg School of Management notes that humans are social by nature. To support his claim, he points to a 1944 study carried out by Fritz Heider and Mary Simmel. Heider and Simmel showed their research subjects an animation depicting two triangles and a circle moving around a rectangular shape. Although they were only presented with shapes, "people [found] it nearly impossible not to construe these objects as human actors, and to construct a social drama around their movements." There is, moreover, physiological evidence that shows that our status as social animals is no accident. For instance, the presence of oxytocin – a neurotransmitter popular dubbed the "love hormone" – in our neurochemistry suggests that we could not simply get rid of others without experiencing this as a reasonable loss, no matter how sophisticated our companion AI are. We can safely say, then, that we will never abandon our preference for other humans.

Single Player vs. Multiplayer

If you play video games, you're familiar with the first choice many games ask you to make: whether you would like to play in single player or multiplayer mode. Basically, you have to decide whether you want to play against another human player or against a canned AI pre-programmed into the game. Many of us opt to play against human opponents when we have the choice, reserving single player mode for when our friends aren't around.

Video game AI is progressing at an amazing rate. The AI developed by Elon Musk's OpenAI startup has recently defeated some of the best players in the world in the game DOTA 2. DOTA 2 is a game that requires strategy, which means that artificial intelligence is beginning to outpace us when it comes to a skill previously dominated by human beings. But what will this mean for gaming? Will we stop playing video games with human opponents when the AI can outsmart and beat us, mimicking the challenge of playing in multiplayer mode? No, we will not. We will continue to play with each other because we like interacting with real human beings, even if the gaming experience itself is virtually the same. We find games more satisfying when they're played with live opponents, and victory is that much more satisfying when it is over another human.

When Ke Jie who lost the game of GO to Google's AlphaGo, he commented that he doesn't want to play with AI anymore because it is too frustrating. When you can't see a way out of the frustration, it sucks all the fun out of the gameplay. The same isn't always true when playing with others. We are more comfortable and playful in our interactions with other humans, and although there is some degree of frustration that comes with always losing, we rarely refuse to play with someone else simply because their skill level far surpasses our own.

Human Discrimination

I am reluctant to use discrimination as a point of defense for my thesis that machines won't replace humans as a class, but it's a fact that must be faced. Humans engage in troubling practices of discrimination. Even when someone is our neighbor, it's not unusual for someone to discriminate against them on some basis – race, religion, economic class. What this discrimination shows, no matter how troubling it is, is that we treat some human beings with respect. We can only discriminate against others if we have in mind a hierarchy of respect.

It's altogether different with machines. It makes no sense to consider whether we can ever treat machines equally, since by definition they are not worth our respect. Would you treat a car as your equal? Would you treat Alpha GO with the same respect you pay to a Grand Master? No, because you know they do not have feeling, they do not gain their status by working hard, nor do they demonstrate their dedication. Human appreciate these attributes, and we confer respect on anyone we deem to have them.

The New Employment Model: Human + AI

Human + AI will be the future face of the employee. Currently, when we are employed by a company, they hire us as a person. We sign ourselves over to go to work for 40 hours a week, use the tools and equipment provided by the employer, and perform the job that has been assigned to us.

In the later stages of the Mind-as-a-Service world, that kind of exclusively human employment will be unheard of. We won't be able to function and produce without our MIA at our side, and that will be as true for our work lives as it will be for our personal ones. Our knowledge, experience, and skills will be integrated with the MIA, making us far more dependent on AI than we currently are.

At this point in the MaaS progression, we can't just separate ourselves from the MIA and go to work on our own. When we step into a job interview today, we sell our ability to help the employer succeed. In the AI evolution, we sell more than that – we will sell our AI capabilities and our ability to orchestrate AI to achieve amazing things. When a company hires us, then, they're really hiring the individual together with their MIA. They are, in essence, hiring employees for their intellectual capabilities and skills – whether those are organic or not. The employment contract, accordingly, will likely stipulate work schedules, productivity targets, and work tasks that simply cannot be performed without the assistance of the MIA. In principle, things won't be all that different. A sushi chef who wants to create the finest dishes for their customers will bring their best knives to work, source the freshest ingredients, and prepare dishes using all of their culinary knowledge, tricks, and their own personal talents. It will be the same for the third stage of Mind-as-a-Service. Like the sushi chef, we will make sure to have the highest quality tools and the best resources available. The only difference will be that our tools will include our MIA. And of course, just as the chef is paid handsomely if they can provide superior results, Human + AI employees will fetch a premium price compared to employees restricted to human intelligence and productivity levels.

The Uber Model

Uber points us to the future, in a way. The company uses a similar model to the one predicted for late-stage MaaS. Like the employee who works using their MIA, Uber drivers actually bring their own car when they go to work. Uber ensures that the car is in proper shape – is in good condition, not too old, and an acceptable model – but they don't actually supply drivers with the transportation. Since this model is so new, there are a number of questions about the details, some of which are currently being heard in courts. One of the more vexing ones has to do with the status of the driver. Are Uber drivers employees of Uber, or are they independent contractors? Uber wants to classify drivers as contractors because they use their own car and aren't on the payroll. But some courts have already decided that Uber drivers are, indeed, employees because they provide a service on behalf of Uber, regardless of who has supplied the vehicle they use to do it.

The concept is similar to Mind-as-a-Service, except that instead of supplying a means of transportation, employees will supply their (enhanced) intellectual power. Naturally, there will be a lot of tricky legal and regulatory issues that arise from this. But with precedents like Uber, we will hopefully have a clearer issue about the status of the Human + AI worker by the time AI technology ushers in this new era of work.

BYOAI (Bring Your Own Artificial Intelligence)

There is already a term to describe this kind of model. It takes the form of "Bring Your Own X." Parties advertised as BYOB (bring your own beer) signaled to attendees that liquor would not be supplied for them. Now, the same concept is used in the business world with BYOD (bring you own device), an acronym that encourages employees to bring their own electronic devices ¬— laptops, tablets, smartphones — to work and use them to perform their jobs instead of being supplied with them. The employer will provide onboarding assistance and policies that facilitate the integration of the worker's personal device into the company system, helping them with network connectivity, email setup, and so on.

The idea is to trust the employee. Rather than supply them with a work device, the assumption is that they can do better, do more, and work more comfortably if they are using the device of their choice. AI is the same; it's just a family of better tools. Since the MIA are associated so tightly with us under the Mind-as-a-Service model, people are already seamlessly integrated with their MIA as one entity. At this stage, it may sometimes be difficult to separate a human from their AI.

The MaaS Class

The BYOAI employment model will have its start as a very strange model in HR departments and the recruiting industry overall. But as we become more intellectually integrated intellectually with AI, it will become a reasonable request. Once AI integration is commonplace and everyone is integrated with AI at various levels of dependency, the ones without extended AI power (those who are deemed "not evolved") will be considered abnormal. Like those who live in the developed world but still don't have cell phones – or who are still stubbornly using a 1990's era GSM phone – those who choose not to enhance their cognitive abilities by outsourcing some of them to an MIA will be hard to come by. I am not saying they won't be able to live a good life; simply that they will be in a small minority.

The working class of the early 21st century, especially those in white-collar occupations, relies on intellectual ability or knowledge to deliver value to their customers. They are the ones who will be most affected by this new model. Those who abstain from the AI evolution will find themselves competing with a new breed of Human + AI workers.

As is the case with every major technological disruption, we can foresee a protectionism developing around human-only employment at first. Those arguing in favor of unenhanced work will claim that AI is unsafe, can't be trusted, and can't deliver the same value that a human can. (Under the nightmare scenario of an AI takeover, they may have a point. They will, however, have a far weaker argument against the Mind-as-a-Service class, since this new class will have the best of both worlds.) Unions and worker associations will lobby to ban AI in the workplace in an effort to protect the job security of non-AI-integrated workers. It will surely be a losing cause; companies will find humans who have embraced the AI evolution to be more employable because they are, in effect, hiring more than one human being. They may be paying a higher salary for their service, but they will more than make that up in the gains in productivity.

There might still be room in the new employment model for human-only services. But they are likely to play the same role that unenhanced work does in our current era. We can, for instance, hire a horse-drawn carriage to transport us across town. It's a great option for a romantic date or just a bit of relaxed fun, but it is otherwise obsolete ¬– if you simply want to get from Point A to Point B in a reasonable amount of time, you'll hail a cab instead (and just about anyone would rather deal with the upkeep involved in owning a car compared to that of owning a horse!) Similarly, many people will pay a premium for artisanal, hand-crafted items. These have a nice, rustic touch to them, but by and large we prefer the affordability and uniformity of machine-produced goods. There might be a similar role for unenhanced human workers in the future. Working with them might give the services a rustic, artisanal, even romantic touch. But anyone – and this will be almost everyone – who wants to have something done efficiently, precisely, and cost-effectively will get their services from a Human + AI worker. Unenhanced jobs, if they do exist, will be scarce. For most people, the only hope of gainful employment will be by using an MIA.

New Business Models

New business models will crop up as Mind-as-a-Service matures and employment models change to keep up with its developments (we'll discuss industry transformation in greater detail in Chapter 6). Currently, we organize businesses according to four models:

B2B (Business-to-Business) – B2B companies are those that perform services for other business entities. Companies like IBM and Oracle, for example, sell enterprise-class technologies and typically do business only with other businesses, since individual customers would rarely need such complex solutions nor be able to afford the hefty price tag that comes along with them. Manufacturers are also usually B2B businesses since they sell to wholesalers rather than directly to consumers.

B2C (Business-to-Consumer) – This is the type of business that consumers interact with every day, including retail stores, gas station, online shops, and even local utility providers. While they likely deal with other businesses (such as suppliers) in some capacity, their business model is based on selling goods and services directly to consumers.

C2C (Consumer-to-Consumer) – This captures consumers who do business directly with other consumers, usually facilitated by a third-party platform. eBay, Craigslist, and other online marketplaces are familiar examples of C2C business models. And, as we saw above, if Uber drivers are considered contractors, then Uber can also be seen as a business operating under the C2C model.

C2B (Consumer-to-Business) – This model is perhaps the least widespread. C2B platforms allow consumers to set prices for the goods they want to purchase. The company selling the product can then make the final decision about whether to sell the item under the proposed terms.

With Mind-as-a-Service, however, two new business models will emerge. I will call them B2A (Business-to-AI) and A2A

(AI-to-AI).

The B2A Business Model

B2A stands for "Business-to-AI," which might strike most people a bit funny when they first hear it. After all, it indicates that the target consumer under this business model is not a human or a corporate entity, but a machine. It is essentially an evolution of B2C, where the consumer is not a human but an AI. Although it might seem odd to us now, under the MaaS model, B2A transactions will be routine.

Now, not just any AI will be able to fulfill a B2A model – your Nest thermostat, no matter how well it can learn your temperature preferences, will not be able to independently engage in a business transaction. Under a B2A model, the AI must, first, have superhuman intelligence and be able to consider different variables and make independent decisions. Second, humans must delegate some authority to the AI, enabling it to make purchases.

The B2A model doesn't just mean that an AI will replace the human consumer in business transactions; it also means that a new market will emerge that solely exists between AI and any business. With the advent of the B2A business model, your MIA could go shopping for its own capabilities. If a carpenter wants to build a wooden cabinet, but their MIA doesn't know how to pick the best type of wood for the project, it can shop for a "wood selector" AI module. The AI will then be able to negotiate costs, integrate the new capabilities with its existing set of skills, and use its newfound abilities without needing any human intervention. Once the service is acquired, and the MIA uses it to identify the ideal materials, then the carpenter can shop for the appropriate lumber. All of this requires a seamless back-and-forth between the AI and various businesses. What this shows is that once humans become Human + AI, the whole dynamic of marketing will change, since it will no longer have to target human decision-makers only.

The A2A Business Model

Businesses interacting directly with AI gives rise to another question: will there also be business transactions involving no humans whatsoever? That will certainly be the case, and we will see a new A2A business model. A2A stands for "AI-to-AI" and it will be an evolution of C2C. Just like the AI has replaced the consumer side of B2C, so it will replace it in C2C.

Essentially, it will be like the C2C marketplaces like eBay and Craigslist, except that instead of humans posting ads, it will be AI listing products and services on these marketplaces on behalf of a human seller or consumer. Then, another AI will search the marketplace for quality product and services.

On the human side, A2A could be like having an MIA butler getting new items for your home while also getting rid of things for you. It may not be intuitive at first, but humans will quickly adapt – we always do when something is incredibly convenient.

At some point, depending on the quality of MIAs and the comfort level of humans, MIAs will be able to do more and more. Say your MIA has a certain set of priorities it runs through whenever it has to buy milk for you – your preferences, expiration dates, whether the product is organic, how eco-friendly the production is, and of course the price. Ready to calculate all of these factors, your MIA will connect with a list of online retailers' AI-only portals (which might only list IP addresses) and figure out which product each retailer has in stock that best meets the precise combination of those factors. The retailer's AI might negotiate with your AI and "convince" it to buy in bulk, or it might offer various deals, such as offering a 20% discount on packaged cookies if they're purchased along with the milk. The two AI continue to quickly go back and forth until your MIA secures a good deal for you, and the other AI has made a sale on behalf of its retailer. (I will have a lot more to say about A2A business models for the retail industry in Part 6.)

New Product Categories

With new business models come new products – just look at all the highly specific, esoteric, and unusual products and services you can find on Craigslist but could never get from a traditional business. (A Craigslist seller even once claimed to be selling a human soul; try finding that at Walmart!) Mind-as-a-Service will likewise create new product categories. There will be a whole new family of tech solutions that exist solely to be consumed by AI.

There will be enterprise-level AI modules that allow them to perform industrial-level automation. With these products, AI can be hired by and integrated within large AI Systems. For example, an AI that could summon and command a fleet of trucks across the Washington DC area at low cost to fulfill a manufacturer's rush order. The AI may be owned or controlled by a few highly skilled MIA-integrated humans who own the trucks and are able to deploy them as needed.

There will also be consumer-level AI that the MIA will engage and integrate with seamlessly. Think about a photography AI that could effectively filter pictures based on the photographer's personal style and artistic touches. Or what about a medical doctor's AI that specializes in both otorhinolaryngology (ear, nose, and throat) and pediatrics? By integrating both specialties into their AI and packaging it as a product, they can provide their expertise through their MIA to parents who need advice or care when their child seems to be having respiratory issues. It's impossible to fully predict what kinds of products we'll see emerging from these new business models, but whatever they are, they are sure to provide incredible convenience and efficiency.

MaaS-AI Integration Technology

Humans communication is complex. We convey our thoughts and emotions, make each other laugh, and supply information by using various verbal and written symbols, as well as bodily signals. Similarly, AI will have its own language to communicate with each other. There won't be an actual, verbal conversation between AI. They won't barter out loud, offering deals and negotiating rates. Instead, there will be an exchange of machine protocols that take place in microseconds. And just like humans as a species speak a variety of languages but as individuals we each only know a handful (if that), AI modules may require translations of their AI languages in order to communicate with each other. An AI may work with a particular set of human data that is not immediately legible to other AI, but can be broken down into an understandable format.

As the technology matures and the AI develops a more sophisticated machine language, MIAs will be able to conduct their own searches for fellow AI, evaluate them in light of their human owners' requirements and preferences, and then integrate seamlessly with it through a shared language.

The New SEO: MaaS-AI Discovery Optimization

Before the internet, we relied on a physical business directory or the phone book's Yellow Pages to help us find out what businesses and contractors were out there. And to expand our professional network, we relied largely on business cards that every company leader would pass out liberally – the LinkedIn of its day. Once we entered the internet age, we gained access to online directories and professional networks that allowed us to do the same things, except more conveniently and often with better results. Since the early 2000s, our habits have changed once again. Search technologies like Google became so popular that the neologism "googling" entered the Merriam-Webster dictionary, and now googling (or using another search engine like Bing) is the first thing we do when we want more information about a business or find out what services are available in our area.

With the information explosion, there is an abundance of information on the web, and every person and business is fighting for attention. One of the best ways to get attention is to master the science of grabbing the attention of search engines. This is done by applying the principles of Search Engine Optimization (SEO), an industry focused on increasing the visibility of webpages (without having to pay a premium to be featured) by strategically using keywords and links to help the site look relevant and authoritative. The industry refers to this visibility as earning "natural," "organic," or "earned" search engine results. This is no trifling matter. The higher the website is ranked in search results, and the more frequently it appears in the search results list, the more visitors it can attract. And the more visitors a company attracts, the more opportunity they have of converting interested individuals into paying customers

SEO is designed to give human users the sites they really want to find. But what will happen to it when businesses (at least B2A and A2A ones) will be hoping to get the attention of AI visitors instead? Under MaaS, SEO will evolve into what I will call AIDO – AI Discovery Optimization. Like human internet users, your MIA will employ search and discovery services, albeit designed specifically for AI. These AI search engines will use algorithms to rank the various services. One difference, however, is that humans consume information in fairly predictable ways, and so long as a search engine can simulate these patterns, it can deliver useful results. That isn't the case for AI. AI can come in many different forms and take on various shapes, depending on how they take in information. Some MIA may be more "logical" than the other, while some will others will be more idiosyncratic, guided by specific sets of values and variables. This will be the next frontier for business competition. Companies hoping to secure a healthy segment of the AI-driven market will have to optimize their sites to capture this new AI online traffic.

Human-AI Integration

As Mind-as-a-Service matures, AI could go through stages of integration. In its earlier stages, MIAs may require their human owners to participate in the search and evaluation process. Since we won't have technology advanced enough to allow genuinely seamless integration with AI, we may still need to issue verbal commands or use actively use some kind of interface to communicate with our MIA. We would issue commands and requests the same way we do now with Amazon's Alexa or Apple's Siri. And like Alexa or Siri, our MIA would engage with us using the language of our choice.

As the technology advances, our active interactions with the MIA will become less overt and less frequent. We might, instead, have a small device attached to the eyeball so that the AI sees what we see so that we don't have to convey that information to it. Or we might go even a step further and enable it to tap into our nerve system and read our emotions so that it knows what kind of novels excite us, who we would rather avoid, and can tell when we are falling in love with someone. There are tons of possibilities, but whatever methods we decide to use they will have the same result: accomplishing more and faster with less and less active involvement.

MaaS AI Hosting

Our MIAs will be powerful algorithms, and their power will multiply when they connect with other AI. Unlike many of the software tools we use now, the MIA will not "live" in our phones or laptops. Very likely it will be "living" in the cloud and communicate with you through some sort of integration device described in the previous section.

Well-functioning hosting services will be critical to the efficiency of your personal AI, and critical for the "life" of your AI. If the hosting service goes out of service, your AI is also out of service. And if you, like most people at that point, rely on your AI to make a living, then you are out of service, too.

When your laptop or smartphone battery dies and there is no charger in sight, it feels like some of your abilities have been temporarily handicapped. And if these devices are essential for your livelihood, being without them might make you feel helpless. Now just imagine how critical our tech tools will be when our dependence on them intensifies. An outage at the hosting service will bring your life to a grinding halt. The Jobs of the Future

New business models, new products, a new employment class – it won't come as much of a surprise when I tell you that there will be new jobs, too.

We will discuss this at greater length in Part 5, but the A2A business model will require be facilitated by the creation of new jobs, including designing interfaces for AI interaction. New types of product designers will also be needed to build new products with different AI modules. When we'll be working with a series of decentralized Mind-as-a-Service AI modules that can be connected, after all, it will give a whole new meaning to "product design." And since the value we get out of our MIA depends entirely on what and how much they can do, AI training and coaching could become a very profitable line of work. Think of what a difference it makes to own a dog who has been with a trainer. They're able to do more, are less aggressive, and can follow commands. Now just imagine how much more crucial a good trainer would be if we relied on our dogs to get our daily tasks done or improve our business efficiencies.

The New Currency of Power

Everyone knows that knowledge is power, but that's never truer than in the age of AI. Knowledge feeds AI in the form of data; it can't function without. Everything happening in the world can be stored in data form and potentially interpreted and understood by AI. That's true of simple data, like what you eat or the items you have stored in your refrigerator. And with that data, your AI can make recommendations to help you improve your health or make sure you don't forget anything you need while shopping. But it's also true of more complex data, like the 5000 years of recorded history of China, the personal changes Adolf Hitler underwent from 1901 to 1940 according to a historian from Ludwig-Maximilians-Universität München, how different elements of the period table react when they come into contact, or the way poodles behave differently than chihuahuas under different climates. These are all sets of data that AI might require when helping us make better decisions, whether it's helping a historian decide which journal articles to read next or helping a parent decide what breed of puppy to get as a surprise to their children.

But what about unstructured data? This type of data is more complex than even the huge stores of more easily quantified and "read" data like the sum of our written historical records. Thy include the drawings of Leonardo da Vinci, blueprints and 3D models designed by the famous Chinese-American architect Ieoh Ming Pei, or even James Cameron's movie Titanic. These provide us with data points that are less clearly organized. They rely more on subjective impressions, aesthetic judgments, and emotional reactions. They are, in other words, the kind of data we learn by absorbing, by taking in. This will be a more challenging form of data to handle, but it won't be impossible. Our MIA will be closely at our side, and they will be able to absorb these forms of data much in the same way we do.

In the world of AI evolution, data will be the new currency of power. The world, after all, will be AI-drive, and AI acts and learns based on data. It will be AI's memory, knowledge, and wisdom. Even now, when AI is still in its relative infancy, we have come to the era of Big Data, where those who control or know how to make use of data are able to shape our world. Some of the entities that have mastered data, like Google, have become among the most influential ones of our age.

Internet of Things (IoT) and Big Data

Data is also a significant player in parts of our lives that we don't always think of as data-rich. The hype around the Internet of Things (IoT) is mostly about data. IoT is essentially connecting traditionally unnetworked devices, like refrigerators or cameras, to the internet. Everything from cellphones and cars to coffee makers, shoes, and lamps can be made part of the Internet of Things.

Smart devices use lots of sensors to collect data in real time and make algorithmic decisions based on it. In fact, the concepts of Big Data and IoT align very closely. Let's talk about thermostats again. If you have a run-of-the-mill thermostat, it will be equipped with a sensor that detects the ambient temperature and then either turns the heat on or off in response. Now, if you have a Nest thermostat, you've dipped a toe into the Internet of Things. Your thermostat does a lot more. It will keep a history of when people are in the room on an average day and use it to adjust to a comfortable temperature when it predicts someone will be entering the room soon. Already, you have a device that collects some key data about your daily routines.

Where does Big Data come in? Well, if your devices — and those of your neighbors — collect enough data, it won't be able to interpret them in interesting ways by relying only on simple logic and relational databases. Processing that much data would simply take too long. By the time the information has been processed and understood by your devices, it will be outdated and of little use. Big Data focuses on managing and understanding these large quantities of data. Specifically, it analyzes data that has four qualities: volume, velocity, veracity, and variety. Let's go over each of those one by one to get a sense of the kind of data we're dealing with today.

Volume. Since the dawn of the internet age, we've created unprecedented amounts of data. In fact, our output is so high that 90% of the data that we have were created in just the last two years. And we haven't plateaued yet: with more apps and sensors running all the time, not to mention the decreasing cost of data storage, we're bound to see this explosion continue.

Velocity. Velocity is the speed at which data travels. There is an estimated 50,000 GB per second of global internet traffic. And as the Internet of Things goes mainstream and more of our devices become connected, we'll need the data to travel quickly and constantly. Investment banks are now using Quants buy and sell stocks based on algorithmic analyses of data. In the future, Quants use more and more minute data to surpass their competitors. For example, an analyst in the retail sector might use large-scale monitoring technologies to get a comprehensive understanding of the foot traffic at each store. Monitoring systems that analyze various details about customers' in-store behavior could also give them a strong estimate of the company's revenue before the company publishes its quarterly report. The more sophisticated their use of data, the more likely they are to beat out their competitors.

Variety. With data constantly being collected from various sensors, monitors, and applications, the variety of data has increased dramatically. We've come a long way from storing numbers and text, and we are now dealing with video, images, and other documents, not to mention the structured data most software applications collect. Looking at the data is not difficult, but understanding and interpreting it are, and we require special technologies to do so.

Veracity. We have huge quantities of data, but its quality matters as well. Veracity refers to how accurate the data are, and how much they can be trusted. It is estimated low-quality data costs the US economy $3.1 Trillion annually. Clearly, this is no small matter.

Better Data Trumps Opinions, Guesses, and Intuitions

Data is the foundation of most AI. The more data they

have, the more complex the decisions they can make. Complexity, however, is only one feature of a good decision-making process. A good process will also use quality data to deliver quality decisions.

Imagine that you're building a house using various building materials like wooden slabs, nails, and insulating materials. To transform that raw material into a house, you'll need a process – in this case, it will involve a blueprint, tools, and construction skills. Now suppose your two-by-fours are of poor quality – say that some aren't quite firm enough, they all have a different texture, their sizes aren't uniform, and they vary in thickness. These difference in the quality of your materials causes the building to be unstable. What can you do to fix it? Building more on top of it won't help, since it won't eliminate the foundational problems.

It's the same with data. If your data are not clean, using it is risky and could become an expensive problem. The data won't clean itself, so you can't keep using it and expect your decisions to get any better. You either need to throw out the bad data and rebuild your database with higher quality data, or compensate for the poor data quality with more sophisticated algorithms that can take its quality into consideration when making decisions (but why do it the hard way if you can simply use good data?)

In the long term, good data trumps everything. Statistically speaking, you will make better decisions by referencing a large amount of good data – the more the better. And it's not just human agents who need it. Thanks to machine learning technology, machine learns from the data they collect. Once that technology advances further, machines could track thousands or tens of thousands of variables at a time and draw predictions based on them. With that many different variables to consider, you can guess how much historic data will be needed. Say you want to decide which of two jobs to take. You have to consider all the data about the jobs, current and recent economic conditions, the locations, the employer, the future of the company, their products, your family, your social circle, and your values. I could keep going, but already we have several factors to consider, each of which will have numerous variables. Based on the information available to you in that situation, you would perform a subjective analysis and come to some conclusion. But the best way an AI can predict which job would work best for you is to find someone (or many people) who has a similar profile as you. They had the opportunities, a similar environment, a comparable social profile. With data about that person's situation before they made the decision and the outcomes of the decision they made, the AI can then make a very educated guess about which job would be the best choice for you. Getting all that information is hard, to be sure, but it doesn't mean that this data doesn't exist. Data Is the New Oil

Data will become even more important in the world of Mind-as-a-Service. Where in the past it was oil that facilitated our use of the most important machinery, in the MaaS era, data will be what enables us to use the most important tools. Your MIA will learn about your past by evaluating your historic data, studying your present data, and comparing the two to understand your growth and change patterns. By owning that data, the MIA essentially has a copy of you, which allows it to truly act on your behalf.

Data will also have a high commercial value. As a consumer, there are two primary ways you will be able to benefit from your data: sell it, or use it to create new products and services.

Selling Your Data

The first way you will be able to benefit from your data is to simply it. The trouble is, it's difficult to sell your own data per se, and companies won't knock on individual people's doors asking if they want to sell it. And, really, they don't need to. It might surprise you, but you have probably been selling your data to corporations without even knowing it.

Most people don't think of using social media platforms as

engaging in a business transaction. After all, you don't pay Facebook or Twitter anything to set up and use an account. But there is a price for accessing the service, and that price is your data. Instead of paying a subscription fee, these companies use your online activities to gather data about you. This data includes details about your daily routines, your interests, your hobbies, who you network with, what kind of relationship you have with your contacts, what you do with your friends, and what kinds of content you feel is worth reposting. From the minute you start using these services, you are handing over details about your life. If you post your Goodreads ratings and reviews on Facebook, it knows what you read. By analyzing the keywords you use, it can know what you're interested in. And, of course, it know (quite literally) what you like.

Companies and advertisers already value your data. And as AI becomes more widespread, your data will become even more valuable. It will also become clear just how powerful your data can be, and people will become more guarded about it. At some point in the future, privacy advocates and social movements will rally around the cause of staying in control of our data, instead of giving it up without clear benefits in return.

In fact, Europe has already started to do this with its General Data Protection Regulation (GDPR). The primary objective of the GDPR is to give citizens control over their personal data, which it does in part by appointing data controllers, data processors, and a Data Protection Officer (DPO) to ensure compliance across all 28 EU member states.

GDPR is just the start of citizens regaining and retaining control of one of their most valuable assets − their data. Services that wish to collect data from its users will have to do so transparently, and people will have the final say in how corporations can use their data. Once AI becomes hungry for data, regular users like you and me will be able to sell our data to companies like Facebook and Amazon. With proper regulation, any service or platform will allow you to disable the collection of your data or request that it stops plugging it into their algorithm, unless they pay you a usage fee. Another option would be for them to charge you for their services if you disable data sharing, but most companies will be hesitant to go down that route. Users are the lifeblood of social networks, and they can't risk losing them by putting up barriers to use.

In the connected age, data will be the new oil. The difference, however, is that you will be the oil well. But of course, not all of the crude oil drilled from the well is equal. In its natural, unrefined state, crude oil varies in density and consistency. Likewise, not all data have the same value. For instance, data about what you bought or ate in the last few weeks is more important than data about what you ate two years ago. Data about which bands you like is more important than data about which numbers you like to play in the lottery. They will, accordingly, fetch a different value if you manage to sell them.

Using Your Data to Create Products and Services

When AI becomes ubiquitous, those with an entrepreneurial spirit can create services using data – theirs and other people's. Remember the third model of Mind-as-a-Service: your mind providing services to others.

When you acquire an MIA, which learns and adapt to you, you are basically sharing your personal data unconditionally. The MIA becomes an extension of you, and your life data defines you and your MIA. Whoever has access to your data has access to your personal and life, as well as your MIA. If you lose control of your data, you lose control of yourself. In doing so, you become obsolete!

If, however, you have secured your personal data, guard it like you would guard any of your other properties. You wouldn't let just anyone use your car, would you? So, why not be careful about who uses your data, too?

One reason it's important to guard your data is that you can use the way large companies use their intellectual property: to create unique products and services that give you a competitive advantage over others.

When you "level up" your MIA by adding AI modules, you are going to give it a very unique expertise. This unique expertise will be very valuable to many companies. For example, an accounting expert can use their MIA to cycle through every possible combination and comb through extensive records to give them powerful investigative force. When you and your MIA know or can do something unique, it can become your livelihood, so keep your knowledge secured

And, moreover, you will be collecting more data specific to your expertise as your MIA provides its services. Just like a human worker, the MIA will become better and better at its job over time. Collecting data will enrich it and allow it to make better decisions.

A Data Chef

Imagine your data as a set of ingredients. When you cook, you will prep your ingredients. You might, first, wash the vegetables, clean the chicken, cut out the useless internal organs of a fish. Then you follow a recipe's instructions and cook the food until it has the right taste and texture. It's the same with data. Your data are your ingredients, and you have to clean them before trying to organize them into a dish.

Not every part of your data will be usable. If you're creative enough, you can make something out of just about any ingredient. It's the same with data. Once you've cleansed it and understand the data, it can be turned into information, just as the chef turns the ingredients into a meal. You can then integrate your information to make it usable for AI or another machine. Your data will be the AI's memory, and your memory combined with the intelligent power of AI can help you become a super intelligent version of yourself.

Data Is Education for AI

Machine learning relies on data, whether it's human- or machine-generated. By studying the data, the machine will learn and improve itself. The data, in other words, are the MIA's education.

We are the sum total of our experiences. And this is what makes education so important: by providing us with edifying experiences, it changes who we are. AI is essentially the same. Its data is its experience. And we can teach our AI to think, feel, and make decisions like us by feeding it data that matches our experiences.

But how are we going to translate our experiences into data and transmit them to our MIA? We could do it academically. By supplying the MIA with our written output like test results, homework data, writing, and reading habits, it can process this information and learn how we think. No one thinks the same way, and academic records are a good proxy for someone's thinking style. Of course, we also want the MIA to think better than we do. If I can't get more than a D on my math homework, I wouldn't want my MIA to replicate that kind of performance. Thankfully, it will always be possible to fine-tune the MIA's thinking so that it becomes a "better" version of ourselves.

We generate a lot of data in our professional lives as well. Every project you've worked on, all the training you've undergone, every performance report and evaluation you've received – these can all be analyzed by your MIA to get a better sense of who you are and how it should handle professional tasks on your behalf. Let's say you're an accountant, your MIA will need to know your best practices for handling certain types of audits (note that these are your best practices, not generic ones). If you're a lawyer, what do you bring to the cases you work on? What are the minor details that other lawyers tend to overlook but you always look for? What type of questions do you ask someone on the stand? All of these define your professional approach, and once your

MIA gets an understanding of it, they can magnify your professional value and expertise by using its intelligence to assist you.

And of course, there's all the social data that we now upload online. With your permission, the AI can comb through your social media accounts to find out what kind of person you are socially and what kind of people you associate with. The AI will learn how you interact with friends, family, strangers, and service people. Whether we realize it or not, we communicate differently with a customer service representative than we do with our next-door neighbor, and your MIA will become sensitive to these small differences. Again, we will not necessarily want the MIA to replicate our behavior with extreme precision. Maybe we tend to come across a bit rude when commenting on corporate social media accounts. Or maybe we have a habit of saying the wrong thing when a friend announces an engagement, a pregnancy, or a death in the family. This is another case in which we might want to fine-tune the MIA so that it communicates to others in our style but without saying anything we regret.

New Investment Vehicles

Giving your MIA access to your personal data will teach it to become like you. But there's another way you can educate it. You can make an investment in your MIA to amplify its capabilities. Let's say you make a living by flipping houses but you don't know much about real estate law. In your line of work, it might be helpful to know a few things about zoning, building codes, and the regulations that govern the transfer of homes from one owner to another. You could spend countless evenings studying the topic and trying to decipher the legal jargon. Or, you could find better ways to spend that time and, instead, purchase a real estate law module for your MIA. Having an MIA equipped with this module is like having 24/7 assistance from a real estate lawyer with 20 years of experience. Not only does it save you the trouble of acquiring the knowledge yourself, but it will know more about it than you ever could by just studying in your spare time.

Your MIA, in other words, will give you the best of both worlds. It will be able to mimic your mode of thinking, your style of communication, and your decision-making processes. But it will also be able to go beyond what you can do, acquiring additional skills and perfecting the ones you already have.

Conclusion

This chapter focused on building and harnessing Mind-as-a-Service AI's expertise, and customizing combinations of AI modules to deliver unique experiences to your customers. We also looked at the central role of data in his process, as the main ingredient of machine knowledge and learning. And naturally, we saw how all of this would shake up the economy, giving rise to new business models and making data one of the key currencies of the MaaS future.

In the next part of the book, we'll dive deeper into these capabilities and discuss the intellectual, emotional, personal, and inspirational capabilities of MIAs.

Brian Ka Chan

PART 4
THE MIND-AS-A-SERVICE DNA

CHAPTER 7
MIA WISDOM

A smart man makes a mistake, learns from it, and never makes that mistake again. But a wise man finds a smart man and learns from him how to avoid the mistake altogether. -Roy H. Williams

In this chapter, you will learn about:

• Wisdom as one of Mind-as-a-Service Intelligent Agents' three major attributes
  • The MaaS intelligence scale
  • The Capabilities of Wise Machines

Recall the definition of AI as human intelligence exhibited by machines. That means that, by definition, AI requires some form of human intelligence in the mix. And that's obvious in the Mind-as-a-Service world, where your MIA can only do such a great job helping you because it replicates your intelligence.

When the topic of human intelligence comes up, most of us turn our minds to IQ. The IQ is an Intelligent Quotient, a score derived from several standardized tests designed to assess human intelligence. Historically, IQ is calculated by taking a person's mental age score, obtained by administering an intelligence test, and dividing it by that person's chronological age, expressed in both years and months. The resulting fraction is multiplied by 100 to obtain the individual's IQ score. When current IQ tests were developed, the median raw score of the norming sample was defined as IQ 100, meaning that an IQ of 100 would track average intelligence, with standard deviations of 15 IQ points on either side. Approximately two-thirds of the population scores within the 85 to 115 range, and about 5 percent of the population scores higher than 125 and another 5 percent score below 75.

Although IQ scores assign a numerical value to an individual's intelligence, these scores are only estimates. Unlike distance and mass, intelligence is too abstract to be measured concretely. Still, they are not entirely arbitrary, which is evidenced by the fact that IQ scores have been associated with morbidity and mortality, parental social status, and appears to be substantially hereditary (although the debate continues to rage about whether inheritance is the true cause of the link these similarities in IQ levels).

Obviously, every one of us will want an MIA with a high IQ (or the machine equivalent). However, high intelligence is not the only attribute we need them to have. Intelligence is only the beginning. The MIA needs to go beyond it and acquire knowledge – and then go beyond that and be smart enough to apply the knowledge. Once it can do that, the MIA will also need to keep track of what the effects of acting on its knowledge and learn from its mistakes. In fact, I envision MIAs being able to learn from other people's mistakes without having to make those mistakes themselves.

Based on this, I will divide the MIA's intelligence into four levels, ranging from the least sophisticated to the most:
1. Basic Intellectual Functions
2. Knowledge
3. Smarts
4. Wisdom

Basic Cognitive Functions

What do I mean by basic Cognitive intelligence? Well, let's think about how we humans develop our intellectual capabilities. Newborns start off with some of the capabilities that most of us carry with us our entire lives. They can register sounds, recognize shapes and colors, and have some spatial awareness. Gradually, we refine these basic capabilities and add onto them.

There are many components of basic intelligence, and different ways of classifying them, too. I won't attempt to create my own system, so I will defer to th American developmental psychologist Dr. Howard Gardner. With slight variation from Gardner's list, here are the seven types of basic intelligence humans possess:
- Logical and Mathematical
- Bodily-Physical (Movement)
- Linguistic
- Biological Classification
- Artistic
- Spatial
- Intrapersonal

Logical and Mathematical Intelligence

Logical-mathematical intelligence is the simplest form of intelligence. It is the ability to calculate, quantify, consider propositions and hypotheses, and carry out complete mathematical operations. It enables us to compare things and perceive relationships and connections between them. It's also what gives us the ability to use abstract, symbolic thought;

sequential reasoning skills; and inductive and deductive modes of reasoning. This is the form of intelligence that you will find unusually well developed in mathematicians, scientists, and detectives. But high levels of it can also be identified in young adults, too, by their interest in patterns, categories, and relationships. Highly logical people are drawn to arithmetic problems, strategy games, and experiments.

Bodily-Physical Intelligence (Movement)

Bodily intelligence is the capability to move objects and apply physical skills properly. It includes moving an object, moving one's own body, or understanding the objects that is being sensed or touched. It's on display in people who have to coordinate their own movements with extreme precision, such as dancers and gymnasts, as well as those who have to manipulate expertly manipulate objects, such as basketball players and sculptors.

Linguistic Intelligence

Linguistic intelligence governs the use and understanding of language, including the ability to use and understand words, express oneself using verbal or written communication, and appreciate the layered and often hidden meaning behind words. Linguistic intelligence allows us to understand the order and meaning of words and to apply meta-linguistic skills to reflect on our use of language. This is perhaps the most widely shared human competence. Poets, novelists, journalists, public speakers, and others who are especially adept at communicating ideas or manipulating language in clever ways display high levels of linguistic intelligence. It is also evident in young adults who enjoy writing, reading, telling stories, or doing crossword puzzles and other word games.

Biological Classification

By biological classification I don't mean the kind of thing

you do in biology class when you categorize living things according to taxa like kingdom, phylum, genus, and species. What I mean is simply the basic intellectual ability to discriminate between living things and their non-living counterparts, such as understanding the difference between trees and the wood that originates from them, and living animals from the fur that they once wore. It also tracks a sensitivity to other features of the natural world, such as clouds and rock configurations. This ability was crucial in our evolutionary past as hunters, gatherers, and farmers. It continues to play a central role in certain professions like botany and the culinary arts. It is also speculated that much of our consumer society exploits this naturalistic intelligence to encourage us to discriminate among cars, sneakers, kinds of makeup, and other products.

Artistic Intelligence

Artistic intelligence is what allows us to create and appreciate musical performances and works of art. Musical intelligence, a subset of artistic intelligence, is the capacity to discern pitch, rhythm, timbre, and tone. These are the abilities that enable us to recognize, create, reproduce, and contemplate music. Composers, conductors, musicians, vocalist, and sensitive listeners all demonstrate these abilities. Interestingly, there is often a connection between music and the emotions, and mathematical and musical intelligence may share common underlying thinking processes. Young adults with this kind of intelligence frequently sing to themselves or absent-mindedly drum rhythms on any object they can get their hands on. They are also usually quite aware of sounds others may miss.

Spatial Intelligence

Spatial intelligence is the ability to think in three dimensions. Its core capacities include mental imagery, spatial reasoning, image manipulation, graphic and artistic skills, and an active imagination. Sailors, pilots, sculptors, painters, and architects all exhibit spatial intelligence. Young adults with this kind of intelligence may be fascinated with mazes and jigsaw puzzles, or spend their free time drawing or daydreaming.

Intrapersonal Intelligence

Intrapersonal intelligence is the capacity to understand oneself and one's own thoughts and feelings, as well as the capacity to use this kind self-knowledge to plan and steer one's life. Intrapersonal intelligence, however, isn't only inward-looking; it involves not only an appreciation of the self, but also some grasp of the human condition. This form of intelligence is highly active in psychologists, spiritual leaders, and philosophers. Young adults with high levels of it may be shy or introverted. They will, however, be self-motivated and very aware of their own feelings.

Knowledge

Once we ascend beyond the basic cognitive capabilities described above, we come to knowledge. A knowledgeable AI would be like a human expert who is very well versed in one or more subjects. The expert knows much of what has been documented in their field, and if it's been taught to you in school, there's a good chance they know more about it than you do. The knowledgeable human will be able to draw instructive and astute classifications among (depending on their type of specialization) scientific history, poets and schools of poetry, and literary genres or periods. The Jeopardy! champion Ken Jennings, for instance, proved himself to be extremely knowledgeable while competing on the game show. Ken has many great talents and skills outside of the game (as evidenced by his wonderful series of children's books), but its his command of a vast mental database of facts, names, dates, and allusions that demonstrate his above-average knowledgeability.

While basic intellectual capabilities allow us to interpret and understand the world around us, but understanding the meaning of that information and drawing connections between pieces of knowledge is a skill on an entirely different scale. An AI using basic intellectual functions can, for example, understand the news broadcast on TV, on the radio, and in print or digital newspapers. But a knowledgeable AI will be able to go one step beyond and connect them together to understand the stories.

To do so, it needs abstract and cognitive functions to form a knowledge graph of items. Currently, IBM's Watson is an impressive but still early example of a knowledgeable AI. Watson is a computer system capable of answering questions posed in natural language. The computer system was specifically developed to answer questions on the quiz show Jeopardy!, and in fact, it even squared off against the champions Brad Rutter and Ken Jennings. In 2011, the Watson computer system beat these two human trivia experts and won the first place prize. How did it do it? Not by simply scanning and interpreting its environment. An AI that could understand the words that Alex Trebek read out would not be able to get very far unless it was also quite knowledgeable. Like Rutter and Jennings, Watson had access to a lot of stored and categorized knowledge, except that instead of it being stored in the neurons of a squishy human brain, it accessed it from 200 million pages of structured and unstructured content, consuming four terabytes of disk storage, including the full text of Wikipedia.

I don't think there is any doubt that IBM's Watson is knowledgeable. Anyone or anything that can win a round of Jeopardy! counts as knowledgeable to me. And an MIA that is knowledgeable will be far more helpful than one that can only register its surroundings. With this kind of AI at our disposal, we will have all the information at hand when we need it.

Let's say you need to prepare a meal for 20 people, and you've promised them Italian food. A knowledgeable AI won't be able to prepare the meal for you, but it will give you easy access to thousands of recipes, with information about where to source the most seasonal ingredients, and find professional help if you need any.

Knowledgeable AI is not complete. For one thing, it relies too heavily on static information from documented knowledge. It has an incredible ability to give you answers based on existing information (just watch Watson at work on Jeopardy!), but it doesn't know how to apply the knowledge itself. For that, you'll need a smart AI.

Smarts

Developing a knowledgeable AI is a great accomplishment because it literally brings all recorded information to your fingertips – but that's it. The next improvement will be to make an AI that is smart. We often use the word "smart" to mean a number of things, including knowledgeability, cleverness, and general intelligence. So what do I mean by smarts if it's something more than knowledge? Compare the smart AI to a freshly minted college graduate getting their first job after graduation. They have lots of knowledge gained through studying, and now they can apply that knowledge in their daily work. After years of work, our graduate has now made many mistakes and has had (hopefully more) successes. A new employee, fresh out of the same degree program, comes to work at the company and is impressed by the first employee's insight into the work. They have the same knowledge set, but the more experienced employee has a much better sense of what will work, what won't work, and has a few tricks up their sleeve to handle unusual situations. So, what makes them so different? The experienced worker has had the ability to use their smarts to learn lessons from every application of their skill and knowledge.

Smarts is the ability to:
1.   Apply learned knowledge
2.   Make situational decisions
3.   Create an experience and monitor its outcome
4.   Learn from experience, successes, and mistakes

Notice that for all its knowledgeability, Watson doesn't display smarts in this way. If Watson is asked a question and retrieves a wrong answer from its database (maybe it misunderstood the intent of the question or it accessed a Wikipedia page with false information), it will make the same mistake if it's asked the same question a second time. It knows a lot, but it simply cannot learn from ongoing experience.

Note also that this is another feature of many experts. It's one thing to know everything there is to know about, say, economic theories, but once you get elected to office and you have to decide how to run your country, how do you know which theory to base your decisions on? In fact, this is the trouble with knowledge. Making the right decision isn't always difficult because we don't have enough knowledge; sometimes it's difficult because we have too much of it and it's not clear how to choose between competing facts, theories, and approaches.

A smart AI will be able assess situations, factor in abnormalities, identify patterns, consider options, consult its own experience, and make a selection or a recommendation based on all this processing. And after making that selection, a smart AI can then assess its outcome. If the results are terrible, it can figure out how to avoid making such a bad decision in the future.

AlphaGO can, on some level, do what a smart AI does, albeit in an extremely narrow domain (the game of GO). AlphaGO can identify patterns in historical games, and then come to understand what makes a good move and how it differs from a bad move. Once it gets better, AlphaGO is able to play against itself to create countless iterations of the game and gain the experience required to improve itself. By doing so, it will avoid repeating its mistakes and will learn what patterns of play are most effective.

A smart AI can become the best in their respective field, the same way AlphaGO managed to conquer its specialty. There is, however, still a limitation to this kind of capacity: the experience it gains is not transferable. AlphaGO – no matter how long it will spend fine-tuning its mastery of the game – will never be able to take that experience and reapply it to a different topic or domain.

Wisdom

Say you're an experienced construction project manager and chief engineer. You've gone through years of training as a civil engineer and you have extensive experience managing large construction projects. But you wake up one morning with a clear and intense realization: your true calling is woodworking. You decide to dive headlong into this pursuit, so you quit your job and start planning a woodwork business that will allow you to make a living building wooden furniture. This will be your first woodworking venture, but you're not entirely green. With 30 years of experience working as a project manager, you know a thing or two about financial accounting and are skilled at long-term planning. So, you apply those skills and draft your business plan. Then, you find that you have quite a knack for designing and building furniture. After all, as a civil engineer you spend so much time drawing blueprints, making construction calculations, and building engineering designs. Applying those skills to your woodworking lets you make elegant and sturdy pieces, all while minimizing waste by using the least amount of wood possible.

That ability to take what we have learned in one domain and apply it across various types of situations is what I consider wisdom. Seeing the same broad patterns across different aspects of your life and noticing how transferable one set of skills or one body of knowledge can be is a complex feat. It requires you to understand the meanings and high-level patterns of various scenarios. Similarly, the ability to generate knowledge and insights out of stories (fictional or factual) is itself an advanced skill and falls under the umbrella of wisdom.

What would it mean for an AI to develop this impressive capability? It would mean that the AI is able to understand the world and grasp the true meaning of things, the structure that is behind the superficial qualities. The wise AI may even be able to do some of our most complex (and mysterious) mental work: understanding jokes, the mood of a story, and even poetry. It could also be more efficient than a (merely) smart AI. A smart AI, as we saw, learns from its mistakes. But a wise AI might be able to avoid mistakes in the first place by learning from mistakes in another domain or by analyzing other people's mistakes. It might, for example, be able to avoid making mistakes when drafting a business strategy, not because it has drafted a successful one before but because it has an extensive knowledge of naval warfare and applies the principles of military victory to the realm of business.

Conclusion

From basic intellectual functions, to knowledgeability, smarts, and wisdom. It is no doubt a very impressive AI that could do it all. And yet, in the world of Mind-as-a-Service, wisdom is not the highest form of artificial intelligence. The highest form of AI will be one that can inspire. We will discuss the inspirational quality of an advanced AI later in the book.

I am purposely avoiding going into a lot of technical detail about creating artificial intelligence. One reason is that there are many smart engineers and scientists out there who can create dozens of different ways to model and build the architecture of intelligences at the different levels I have described above. But another reason is that we are still at a very early phase of the Mind-as-a-Service journey. There is simply no how-to available for building such a super-intelligent system, and any attempt to draft one would involve assuming too much and would result too many premature guesses. This book is intended to be an honest discussion about a powerful AI positioning framework, not a technical manuscript that gives us a blueprint for building it.

CHAPTER 8
CHARACTER, ETHICS, AND PREFERENCES

Character is higher than intellect. A great soul will be strong to live as well as think.
- Ralph Waldo Emerson

In the previous chapter, we discussed the several levels of intellectual maturity and complexity that go into creating sophisticated Mind-as-a-Service Intelligent Agents (MIAs). In this chapter, we will flesh out the MIA's characteristics by discussing:

- Preference integration
- Character adoption
- Ethical control

Preference Integration

Understanding your preferences is one of the MIA's most important capabilities. We use intelligence itself whenever we need to make a decision, but we are not machines. Humans are not fully logical, and we don't always base all our reasoning on logical deductions and inferences. In almost every single case, we draw on something fuzzier, something more personal: our preferences.

Take the decision to get a tattoo, for example. I might think that it's a good idea to get one on the back of my neck because the people I know – those I consider to have good taste, anyway – will probably like it. I consult my friends and they support the idea because they think it will make me look cool. When I see people with neck tattoos, I get jealous. But when I see someone with a tattoo on their arm – meh. It will cost the same either way, so the only logical way to maximize the $600 I'm going to put down for my tattoo is to put it somewhere that everyone can see and notice, not somewhere that can be covered by a sleeve.

Am I being logical in making that decision? Yeah, definitely. But would an AI built to satisfy thousands of consumers give me the same result? Definitely not. It would churn through the data and recommend that I get a tattoo in the most popular location (arm? Wrist? Ankle? Perhaps, but definitely not a neck tattoo.) That doesn't mean AI is hopeless; we just haven't built one that is sufficiently personalized yet.=

You might be worried about your privacy. If an ecommerce site had a form asking you to share your deepest, darkest, and weirdest secrets, you probably wouldn't fill it out (or, you'd make something up to protect your innermost thoughts). That's the beauty of Mind-as-a-Service. Your AI will be intimately linked with you and act as an extension of your brain. It will be built to keep secrets for you, with no chance of sharing them under any circumstances. Unlike the imagined ecommerce form, you won't have to even worry about some data entry clerk blushing when they come across your list of preferences. The MIA is loyal to you and only you. It's not like a social network that gives you access to a service in exchange for mining and using your data for its benefit. It doesn't work for the government, your employer, or your spouse. It will only work for you.

As organic beings, we have our own unique set of experiences, and this colors our view of the world. When we're sitting next to someone, looking at the same thing, we both see it differently. We all have our private inner world, and it's through it that we filter everything we encounter.

All of these things shape our preferences. The smallest things can end up guiding our big choices. You want a mini-van but you'd rather not drive a Dodge Caravan. Why? Fuel efficiency? Safety features? No: you've simply seen too many of them when you drop your son off to soccer practice and you don't want to drive the same model as everyone else. Or it could be the other way around: you have a strong desire to fit in, so you'll buy a Dodge Caravan precisely because it's the one you see everywhere. Food's a big one, too. You love sushi, but you think of it as a summer food. When winter comes around, you don't like to eat anything cold, so you spend a few months not ordering any. But then you have a friend with whom you have a lot in common, but on this you're total opposites. She eats sushi all winter because she can't stand the thought of eating raw ingredients that have been transported in the heat of the summer. And the cold doesn't bother her – she even orders ice cream in mid-December. Neither of these preferences are wrong. And if you asked an AI that is keyed into the preferences of the general population whether it's a good idea to eat sushi in the winter, its answer will either disappoint you or your friend.

For your MIA to make useful decisions on your behalf, without needing constant correction from you, it will need to capture your preferences, and potentially share it with all the third party MIAs you use. When your MIA connects with the AI that will order groceries or the AI that will prepare your meals, it will know whether this is a good sushi month for you or whether it should leave the short-grain rice out of the shopping cart.

Whether and how you will share your preferences with your AI is another topic of discussion. You could open yourself up to the MIA so that it can register everything you eat, what you wear, and how you feel about certain things. Gradually, it will come to learn your preference profile. Or you can proactively train your MIA using some sort of questionnaire. This will be handy if you need the MIA's help sooner rather than later, but be warned that the questionnaire will be a very long one.

Character

To really understand you, your MIA will have to know your character. Character is a broad term. It means more than just your preferences, and includes attributes and features that distinguish you as an individual. It's what makes you, you. When someone decides to be your friend or your romantic partner, it's not because they like your preferences (though that can come into play, too); it's because they're drawn to your character.

Goodness is about character – integrity, honesty, kindness, generosity, moral courage, and the like. More than anything else, it is about how we treat other people. - Dennis Prager

---

Before we discuss how an MIA can adopt our personality, let's take a step back and discuss how humans assess each other's personalities in the first place.

There have been tons of studies on human character and

personality over the last two hundred years. In the course of those two centuries, we have developed many tests to measure, classify, and understand individual character and personality traits. These tests are usually referred to as personality assessments and they are self-reported questionnaires that measure your preferred or typical way of being. These assessments are usually divided into two broad categories: tests that are trait-based and those that are type-based.

Trait-Based Assessment

A trait is a characteristic pattern of behavior that is universal, meaning that it shows up across different situations. If you're a dependable person, that's a trait you will exhibit at work, with your friends, and with your children. A trait is also relatively stable over time. No one is considered a patient person because they dealt with setbacks patiently but only over the course of a 72-hour period – that's a fluke, not a trait. Trait-based assessments try to measure and quantify the presence of key traits in order to paint a picture of the individual's character.

The most popular trait-based assessments are those that measure the Big Five traits. factor personality test. These tests place the person on a continuum for each of the following five traits:

Openness to experience (inventive and curious vs. consistent and cautious). Openness reflects the degree of intellectual curiosity, creativity, and preference for novelty and variety that a person has. This trait determines whether the individual is willing to take risks and try new things or prefers to be prudent and comfortable with routine. High openness can be perceived as unpredictability or lack of focus and can manifest itself in the pursuit of self-actualization through intense, euphoric experiences. Those who score lower on this scale tend to gain fulfillment through perseverance and may b more pragmatic and data-driven. They may be perceived as dogmatic and closed-minded.

Conscientiousness (efficient and organized vs. easy-going and careless). Conscientiousness measures a person's dependability, self-discipline, and how sensitive they are to the demands of duty. Highly conscientious people are well organized and habitual planners, and may be accused of being stubborn or obsessive. Those who are lower on the scale, on the other hand, are more flexible and spontaneous, following their whims rather than following procedures. To the conscientious, they may appear sloppy, disorganized, and unreliable.

Extraversion (outgoing and energetic vs. solitary and reserved). Extraversion tracks a person's sociability, gregariousness, and tendency to seek the company of others. Those who rank high on this scale are far more likely to feel confined if they are alone at home and will strongly prefer going out to see people at a bar than staying home to watch a movie or read a book. They may be perceived as attention-seeking or domineering. Those with low extraversion, however, are more reserved and reflective. They are comfortable spending time by themselves and don't feel the need to constantly engage with others. Those who rank especially low on the scale can, however, be perceived as aloof or self-absorbed.

Agreeableness (friendly and compassionate vs. challenging and detached). This trait tracks the difference between a compassionate and cooperative person and a more suspicious and antagonistic one. It is also a measure of our trusting and helpful nature, and whether we are generally well-tempered or not. High agreeableness can be seen as naive or submissive, while low agreeableness personalities are often competitive or challenging, which can be seen as argumentativeness or untrustworthiness.

Neuroticism (sensitive and nervous vs. secure and confident). Neuroticism tracks emotional stability, impulse control, and the tendency to experience unpleasant emotions easily, such as anger, anxiety, and depression. A high need for stability manifests itself as a stable and calm personality, though it can be seen as uninspiring and unconcerned. A low need for stability, on the other hand, makes for a reactive and excitable personality, often very dynamic individuals but possibly more unstable or insecure.

Typed-Based Assessment

Instead of breaking personality down into individual traits, we can think of personalities as types. These types are collections of traits that cluster together to form a person's character. Psychological Types describe healthy differences between people, and will not usually explain or measure competence, skills, excellence, natural ability, or psychological problems. Type-based assessments categorize people into groups based on bi-modal qualities, rather than continuums (meaning that you cannot be both introverted and extroverted, for example). These assessments don't measure how much of a trait an individual has; rather, it will identify the ones that are more pronounced.

The Myers Briggs Type Indicator (MBTI) is the most famous of the type-based personality assessment. It is based on Carl Jung's theory of types, which holds that individuals are either introverts or extroverts, and their behavior and the way they process information follows from these inborn psychological types..

The Myers-Briggs test evaluates personality types and preferences based on the four Jungian psychological types:
- Extraversion (E) or Introversion (I)
- Sensing (S) or Intuition (N)
- Thinking (T) or Feeling (F)
- Judging (J) or Perceiving (P)

This is the personality scale that people refer to when they give themselves four-letter designations. If someone ever tells you, "I'm INTJ," they're referring to the Meyers-Briggs.

Adopting Your Character

Compared to the drawn out process of learning your preferences across various situations, it will be relatively easy for your MIA to adopt your personality.

At a high level, your MIA can simply administer one of

these personality tests to you (or come up with its own answers observing your conduct). In no time, it will know whether it's dealing with an extrovert or an introvert, or how strongly you rank in conscientiousness. In fact, with the right algorithm, your MIA should be able to use a variety of tests and measures to get a very comprehensive picture of your personality. It might not have to restrict itself to the Big Five and, instead, measure dozens of your personality traits. And it could have a more fine-grained set of traits than the Myers-Briggs test.

Once it knows you and your character, the MIA will be able to customize its services to you based on your character traits. Let's say it discovers that you are very risk averse, then it might set your alarm clock early — even if you might up ready to go to the office an hour early. And if it learns that you're an introvert, it might schedule your day in so that it doesn't involve too much social interaction or small talk. Your services will be truly customized, and you won't have to tell the MIA what you want — it already knows you just as well (or better) as you know yourself.

Ethics

Ethics is the moral principles that govern a person's behavior and guides their life plans. They are our standards for what is right and wrong.

The idea of AI ethics is far from new. In Isaac Asimov's 1950 novel series I, Robot, the writer introduces readers to the three laws that govern every robot in this imagined future:

1.   A robot may not injure a human being or, through inaction, allow a human being to come to harm.

2.   A robot must obey orders given it by human beings except where such orders would conflict with the First Law.

3.   A robot must protect its own existence as long as such protection does not conflict with the First or Second Law.

These laws serve as principles by which the robots organize their priorities, and because of which they consider certain actions forbidden. In a nut shell, human safety is the guiding principle, followed by order and productivity, and then self-preservation. Later, Asimov added a fourth, or zeroth law, that had a higher priority than his original three:

0. A robot may not harm humanity, or, by inaction, allow humanity to come to harm.

In many situations, these laws will function just fine. But problems arise when the choice isn't always so clear. Should a robot hurt a person to put a stop to an action that has a 45% chance of harming five people? Does AI ethics it really all come down to math and probability? That's the question.

It would be very difficult to have an AI that follows a strict, rules-based moral code. I question whether such a thing is even possible. There are simply too many grey areas to determine what is right or wrong in a given situation, how much intent matters in a particular context, and how heavily we should weigh consequences. A human being who believes it is wrong to kill might just pull the trigger to take the life of a mass murderer about to detonate a bomb. A robot programmed to never kill a human being might not be able to work through the nuances, and the bomb might go off. Allowing so many people to be killed seems to run counter to the intent behind the rule against taking a human life, but that would be lost on a machine with such strict programming.

Another problem with such delineated, rule-based ethics is the question of who will get to choose the moral principles. Who will be in charge of programming the AI's moral code? What if the owner of the MIA has reprehensible moral views? What if they don't believe human life is important? If the MIA takes on their personalities and preferences, they might start acting on a perverse moral code. What if the AI not only fails to put a stop to the bomb-making mass murderer's plot, but actually assists in creating the bomb?

We will want an MIA that can match our preferences and take on our personality. But it's clear from this problem that we want to make sure that it doesn't just simply adopt just anybody's moral code. Like all other important technologies or substances, we'll need a governing body to enact certain ground rules for AI and enforce those regulations (we'll discuss this in greater detail in a subsequent chapter on regulations).

CHAPTER 9
EMOTIONAL INTELLIGENCE

Your intellect may be confused, but your emotions will never lie to you. -Roger Ebert

When I speak of an AI's emotional capabilities, I don't mean its ability to exercise emotional control (a rather useless ability for a machine). Nor do I mean to speculate about the possibility of building machines with emotions. No, what I mean by it can be roughly captured by emotional intelligence. Emotional intelligence (popularly known as EQ) is a relatively recent concept, dating back to 1995 with the publication of Dan Goldman's book Emotional Intelligence.

In the MaaS context, programming emotional intelligence into the MIA serves as the complete and final stage of the Human-AI Evolution. An emotionally intelligence MIA will be able to read your emotional needs and states, and make decisions for you based on your mood and affect.

In this chapter, you will learn:
- How decisions are affected by our irrational brain
- Mind-as-a-Service emotional monitoring
- Needs, wants, and spontaneous decisions
- How your MIA will guide you through life

Thinking with Emotions

If our MIAs are truly going to be extensions of ourselves, able to act as our surrogates when it comes to decision-making, then they will need to be aware of our emotions at any given time.

Historically, philosophers and economists have underestimated the role emotions play in our decision making (and many still do!) The field of psychology, however, has provided us frameworks for understanding the role emotions play in our thought processes. In his celebrated 2011 book, Thinking, Fast and Slow, psychologist Daniel Kahneman gave us a useful way of thinking about emotional thought processes. According to Kahneman, we use two systems in our thinking. System 1 (OS 1) thinking is intuitive– fast, automatic, and emotional. It is based on rules of thumb (heuristics) and mental patterns (cognitive biases) that result in impressions, feelings, and inclinations. System 2 (OS 2) thinking is the more rational thought process – slow, deliberate, and systematic. It is based on careful evaluation of evidence and rationale, and results in logical conclusions.

So far, the kinds of intelligence we have discussed have been System 2 styles of thinking. It is based on cold, disinterested evaluation of the information available. That will certainly be critical, but we all rely on other types of considerations when making choices. Even those who rely mainly on System 2 thinking will often make use of System 1 processes – they will simply follow their gut, or consider what they're in the mood for. And most of us switch back and forth between the two depending on the situations.

When we extend our brain with an MIA, we will have to

make a choice about how we want the extension to behave. Perhaps we are prone to being flighty and impulsive, and would like our MIA to help us make more reasoned, cautious decisions. By programming the MIA so it demonstrates Systems 2 thinking, it can act as a kind of intellectual conscience, helping us make less emotional decisions. There are a few advantages to steering our decisions toward more logical conclusions. For one, it can help us avoid certain cognitive biases ¬–anchoring, the sunk cost fallacy, confirmation bias, the Dunning-Kruger effect, and the just world hypothesis, to name only a few. A highly logical MIA can help us avoid these tracks and make us less susceptible to marketing tricks and persuasive tactics.

None of those advantages mean that we would never want an MIA whose decision-making processes were aligned with Systems 1 thinking. We may just simply enjoy and respect who we really are, and would like an MIA that can act in the exact ways we would, even if it can be less than fully logical at times. For our MIA to do this, it will be able to have a firm grasp of our real-time emotional and mental states.

Emotional Assessment and Monitoring

Before advising us and recommending anything, our MIA will need to monitor and assess our emotions. There are couple ways that can be done.

One approach is to monitor biological indicators, such as heart rate or the flow of hormones in the bloodstream. An elevated pulse, for example, could signal that you are afraid, excited, or angry. Given contextual clues, the MIA would be able to know which of these emotional states have caused the change in vital signs. The assessment doesn't always have to go so deeply; they could also be based on external observations. The MIA might notice that you are blushing during an interaction with someone. Or it might notice that you're getting goosebumps when you hear a strange sound at night. And again, by using contextual clues it could tell whether you're blushing from embarrassment or because of you've had one too many cocktails.

Another approach is to learn from your direct input. At various points of time during your MIA adoption, you would simply notify it of your emotional state. By telling the MIA when you are happy, angry, or sad, your MIA could establish an emotional database that identifies certain situations as causes of particular emotions. One disadvantage to this approach is that it might result in skewed or imperfect results. Specifically, the MIA might acquire too slim a record of your negative emotions, because you likely wouldn't be in the mood to log your emotions when you're grieving or in a state of depression.

Emotional Responses

Building a profile of your emotional states will be one of part of the MIA's emotional intelligence. The other will be to understand your emotional reactions, that is, how you function while experiencing certain emotions. Our emotional reactions are one of the things that make us unique on an individual level. We may all feel anger at an insult, but some of us will ruminate over it quietly and privately, some will respond with an insult of our own, and others still will not hesitate to throw a punch. It's not enough, then, for the MIA to read our emotional state; it also needs to know what kind of response we would find appropriate given our emotional state.

Let's say you're under stress because of an upcoming interview. Your MIA recognizes this and will jump into action by providing you support. But what will that support look like, exactly? Will it be helping you prepare talking points and interview techniques? Will it be clearing your evening schedule so you can have a long bubble bath to help you relax? Or will it be to queue up a really engrossing television series so you can keep your mind distracted until the big day? Or will it coordinate with your mom's MIA to find a good time for you to call her and talk about your worries? Different approaches work for different people, and the MIA will need to know how we react to stress if it is going to help us handle it.

The emotional intelligence of the MIA can also help you be a more logical thinker. Let's suppose you are prone to the sunk cost fallacy. This is the tendency to view things not worth giving up if you've already put some money, time, or effort into them. It's what might make you decide not to buy a nicer house at a lower price because you've already spent so much of your money fixing up the one you live in. Instead of seeing the two options objectively – the cost of your house compared to the cost of the nicer one – you factor in the costs already spent and give them too much weight. Now, if your MIA knows that you are prone to this kind of fallacy, it can pre-emptively identify potential sunk costs and advise you not to factor them into your decision making. Even a simple reminder like "Don't pass up Option B just because you invested time into Option A" could help us think twice before falling for this fallacy. Or maybe your problem is the opposite and you're likely to give up too quickly. Your MIA could step in before you make an irreversible decision on a whim to tell you, for example, "Don't throw away a two-year relationship just because a good looking stranger gave you a wink!"

With emotional capabilities, the MIA can read our emotions and either work with them to make the kind of intuitive, mood-based decisions we do, or it can help us make choices that aren't so strongly influenced by our quick, emotional responses. An MIA with EQ will allow for either option.

The Subconscious Mind

Only one sixth of the brain's activities happen at the conscious level. There are lots of mysterious, subconscious activities going on in our brains at all times. While they're not always evident to us, our subconscious mental activity does result in patterns that can be learned by observation. Your subconscious mind is essentially a vast system that stores and retrieves data. Its job is to ensure that you respond in the ways you were programmed to respond. Everything you have learned, heard, and seen changes your memories and changes your subconscious mind. You aren't always able to retrieve this subconscious data and you may not always notice it affecting your emotions and behavior, but it's there and has a strong influence on you.

Phobias are a great example of the way subconscious patterns work. Let's say you opened your closet door when you were four years old and were frightened by the rubber snake your brother placed in it as a prank. Since then, you've been afraid of snakes and anything that even resembles a snake. It's irrational – you are aware that many snakes are perfectly harmless – and you may not remember the event itself, but nevertheless it has a powerful influence on your behavior.

Because of its nature, we won't be able to simply answer a survey and give our MIA a complete picture of our subconscious mind. But by analyzing patterns in our behavior and emotional responses, the MIA could learn a lot about what goes on beneath the surface. Of course, it's unlikely that parents will purchase an MIA for their newborns so that they can have an AI that has monitored them from birth (there would be far too many issues related to privacy, voluntary choice, and complexity). And it's even more unlikely that we'll one day find some way to upload our minds – subconscious and all – to a machine. The MIA will, instead, have to read all of our surfaces cues and infer from it what it can. We will want an AI that is a part of us in a very real way, but the subconscious mind will always be an at least partial obstacle to this perfect integration. Even with these limitations, however, the MaaS AI will be able to gain a sophisticated (though not complete) understanding of its owner.

Conclusion

The subject of an MIA's emotional intelligence is a more complicated one than its intellectual capabilities. We will surely want our MIAs to have as high an EQ as they have an IQ, but how we will want them to use it is another question entirely. While its intellectual abilities will be put in service to making optimal decisions on our behalf, it's not clear how each of us will want the MIA to use its emotional intelligence. We might want it to act in accordance to our personal emotional profile, or we might want it to help us keep our emotions in check. Regardless of our choice, however, its ability to read our emotions will matter quite a lot.

These emotional capabilities, however, are where we run into additional problems. Not only are there additional obstacles – ethical, practical, technological – to collecting our emotional data, but privacy concerns are intensified when it comes to measuring our emotional states. We will tackle these thorny issues in greater depth when we get to the chapter on government regulation.

For now, however, we have one more MIA attribute to cover: inspiration. An inspirational MIA is one that is supportive, inspiring, and focused on helping us become a better person. It is another leap of AI technology required, and the closest we can reasonably come to developing an Artificial General Intelligence.

CHAPTER 10
INSPIRATION

In this chapter, you will learn:

• The advanced stage of the Mind-as-a-Service Intelligent Agent's maturity
• Countering AI with AI
• AI creativity, strategy, and inspiration

• How a better world leads to better evolution

Have you been inspired before? You probably answered yes, even though you might not have a clear idea of what you mean by inspiration. So, let's start by giving it some definition.

I take inspiration to be that by which we are moved to act, feel, or think something. It's what happens when something you hear, see, or touch allows you to uncover something you didn't realize before. It happens when someone says something that sparks an idea in you. Or when you witness someone standing up for themselves and it moves you to a similar act of bravery. And it's an experience very familiar to artists, who might happen to glance at the wind shaking the leaves on a tree and rush to their canvas with a fresh idea for a painting.

Most of us like to be inspired. We want to discover new things and enjoy feeling stimulated, which is why inspiration feels so thrilling. We also have our moments of weakness that we want to overcome, so we welcome encouragement and feel a relief when we are inspired to act in line with our values.

Inspiration is also big business. Every year, readers looking for inspiration spend billions on motivational books, and people are willing to spend even more to attend an event by a motivational speaker. Why would so many of us go out of our way to seek inspiration in this way? I can think of a few reasons.

1.   *To reaffirm your faith in hard work and miracles*

Motivational speakers and inspirational books are most effective when they combine real life anecdotes with working wisdom. These tales show the readers and audience that life is a mix of hard work, smart work, miracles, and luck — but never any one of these alone. If you have been working hard and aren't always convinced it's worth it, you may heave a sigh of relief by reading these books and their promise that something good will happen to you.

2.   *To know that failure is a normal part of life*

Many people will seek out self-help and personal development material when they're in a bit of a crisis.

Experiencing a setback can be very discouraging, but a motivational speaker can help you see it not as an insurmountable obstacle, but rather as a stepping stone to your coming success. These positive affirmations are likely to leave you in a better state to deal with failure and the pitfalls that life throws at you.

3.   *To learn from others.*

Mistakes can be great teachers, but their lessons come at a price. Recovering from a mistake can take a lot of time and resources. For that reason, learning from a mentor is often the better way to learn. Motivational stories can help us learn from another person's mistakes so we don't have to suffer through the entire process ourselves. Reading about someone spending fifteen years earning a high income in a soul-crushing finance job before finally quitting to pursue their dream of becoming a graphic designer can help you avoid the painful mistake of spending more than a decade doing the wrong thing for a living. To know you're not alone

Motivational speakers and self-help books can help put your challenges into perspective by presenting you with stories of other people whose mental and emotional conditions may be similar to yours. You can feel a bit of relief knowing that what you're going through is normal, that you're not alone in your struggles but are sharing them a million others. You can also multiply your happiness by knowing that many other people across the globe share the same delights as you do.

4.   To wake up happy every day

An inspired life and a motivated state of mind are often accompanied by surges of happy hormones. Finding constant sources of inspiration can help you wake up each and every morning with a mission, determination, and a smile on your face. That alone is one reason many people seek out inspirational books or motivational speakers.

The tricky thing with inspiration is that you can't really control it. It's not as simple as simply declaring "I want to be inspired" and then letting the inspiration and motivation wash over you. But it's so rewarding that people are willing to spend a lot to get some of the results discussed above. There are no guarantees, of course. They may get those results, or they may not. But listening to motivational speakers is a good way to increase your chances.

What if you could increase your chances of being inspired, too? Not by reading books but by someone you like, or even by yourself? Sounds good, huh?

The Inspirational AI

Inspiration is the fourth attribute of a Mind-as-a-Service Intelligent Agent. After acquiring the ability to process and make decisions on your behalf using basic intellectual functions, then gaining awareness of your preferences and limitations, and becoming familiar with your emotional reactions, the MIA can create ideas based on your needs and wants.

How does an inspirational MIA work? Your MIA will be in tune with your emotional states and thought patterns. When it sees you going through a crisis of faith or simply facing up to all the bad luck you've experienced in your life, it will be able to curate the right material to give you the strength of will you need. Whether it's movies about people who have triumphed over their adversity, articles on how to face adversity in the most productive ways, or novels and poetry that inspire perseverance, your MIA will know just what to prescribe to get you out of your slump.

When a life event comes your way that you don't know how to handle, the MIA will be able to guide you through it. When your partner breaks up with you, you get laid off from your job, or a loved one passes away, the MIA will predict your emotional reactions to these events and know how to best manage them. It might take the initiative to notify a love one that you might need some support. Or it could find the photos and diary entries that you will want to revisit. And it could also know what kind of self-care you need in these situations and work to make it happen, say by planning a cross-country road trip or clearing what it can from your schedule to make more time for reflection.

But an inspirational MIA won't have to wait for you to come into some sort of spiritual or personal difficulty before it springs into action; it can take proactive steps to keep you inspired on a regular basis. It might, for example, comb through podcasts and radio shows to find inspirational stories to play for you after your morning alarm clock rings you awake. This will help you start every day with the right state of mind. It could also deliver inspiration on an as-needed basis, say when your vital signs reveal that you're starting to feel stressed out.

The Observational Companion

Building an inspirational AI is a complex task, and the MIA will require quite a few capabilities before it can meet this need for us. One of them is the skill of observation. By this I don't mean the simply ability to see what is going on around it — observation, in the sense I mean it, requires much more than just a video feed. For one thing, an observational AI would have to be able to tell the difference between various things. It would need to register changes in your routine, for instance, and also to get some sense of whether the change is significant or simply resulted from you being in a rush after sleeping in. It must also be able to recognize the complex significance of losing your job or your partner — not only what it does to your earnings and your Saturday nights, but also the ways that it might make you feel humiliated, insulted, or hurt. Since it is beyond my technical expertise, I won't attempt to discuss the designs of such system. I will leave that task to some of our most brilliant scientists.

The Creative Machine

Creativity is a central part of inspiration, so an inspirational

AI will have to display some creative functions. I don't mean that the AI will need to work through millions of combinations and, through trial and error, discover the optimal ones. What I mean is that your AI should be able to cycle through these various combinations and work them out in its "head" to come up with the ideal one. Let's say it your MIA uses its EQ to assess you and finds that you are feeling bored with your life and have been watching a lot more television shows over the last two months. Your MIA will then work out possible ways to cheer you up. There are many things the MIA could do, from secretly setting you up on a blind to suggesting that you meet up with your high school buddies to reconnect. It will then process every choice, taking into account your own personal preferences and your emotional responses in the past, and pinpoint the one that will best lift you out of your funk.

The danger of highly creative AI

Highly intelligent machines are incredible tools, but they can also be very dangerous. Once we've developed a creative AI, we might lose our last claim to superiority over machines when it comes to thinking and cognitive processes. We can outsmart machines because they are purely logical and there is always some logical loop hole that we can exploit to gain or regain control over AI. But with creative AI, we reach a tipping point in human existential risk. If we can keep the reins and continue to control creative AI, the human race will flourish. But if we lose our control over it, some of our worst fears will come true: we will become obsolete.

Conclusion

Inspirational ability is the most complex attribute of the Mind-as-a-Service MIA. It is also the one that brings us closest to artificial general intelligence. With it, however, comes the real danger of making ourselves obsolete by giving machines the ability that once ensured we were superior to them.

The threat is real – many of our technological visionaries, including Bill Gates, Stephen Hawking, and Elon Musk, have alluded to it – but it's not immediate. There is time left to prepare for this development before the technology catches up with us. And this is the main reason I have designed the Mind-as-a-Service framework, to ensure that AI will be our partners, not our competitors. Naturally, this will take leadership and protection from government entities. That will be the subject of the last part of the book. Before we look at that future, however, we will spend the next part of the book discussing the present, and how everything we have on the market currently maps onto the progression of AI from its current state to its MaaS maturity.

Taming Artificial Intelligence

159

Brian Ka Chan

PART 5

MIND-AS-A-SERVICE AI CLASSIFICATION

CHAPTER 11
MIND-AS-A-SERVICE AI CLASSIFICATION

The vision must be followed by the venture. It is not enough to stare up the steps – we must step up the stairs." -
Vance Havner

Evolution happens over the course of millions of years of trial and error – different mutations and behaviors enter the scene and only the fittest survive. What that fitness means differs across species, whether it's a caterpillar changing its colors to appear like the head of a poisonous snake when it's scared or a gliding possum gliding between trees to evade predators. Thanks to evolution, species have continued to become more efficient at gaining sustenance, protecting themselves, and surviving harsh conditions, and as new threats appear, species seem to find a way to counter them.

As the most intelligent species on this planet (so far, at any rate), we have used technology to speed up evolution. We have manipulated our own DNA instead of waiting for natural evolutionary processes to do it for us. We have even modified other species to suit our needs, including making bananas easier to eat by shrinking their seeds down to such a small size that we can't taste them. We even cross-breed flowers so they last longer for our aesthetic pleasure. These are all instances of what I consider to be planned and forced evolution.

When we guide our own evolution, we do so with a purpose. We have a clear goal that we want to accomplish, and we put our best technology in service of achieving that goal. While it all sounds laudable on the surface – we typically aim at improving our sources of nutrition and making ourselves more intelligent and better able to resist disease – we are playing God and this always comes with some risks. If we want to make sure that our technological upgrades don't go out of control, we need a clear path that guides our evolution in the right direction. Mind-as-a-Service is all about speeding up the human intellectual evolution through a guided Human-AI evolution. Mind-as-a-Service includes a system of human-centric AI classifications that guide the AI's development so it results in a benefit to human beings. This classification can be used to coordinate product managers and product designers to ensure that they all work toward a concerted goal: human-centric artificial intelligence.

The Mind-as-a-Service AI classification is intended as a comprehensive reference model for state-of-the-practice process improvement. It contains important criteria for building future-looking AI products. The Mind-as-a-Service AI classification also completes the MaaS framework by connecting all previous and current AI technologies, mapping their development on a scale of AI maturity, and pointing the way to Artificial General Intelligence.

The MaaS AI Classification

The Mind-as-a-Service AI classification presents eight levels of functional capability and maturity. Each level is characterized by increasingly complex displays of intelligence. In keeping with the principles of MaaS, all levels are human-centric.

Level	Name	DESCRIPTIONI
0	No Intelligence	No intelligence exhibited of any kind (hammers, books, typewriters)
1	Dumb AI	Exhibits the simplest kind of automation (calculators, thermostats, anti-skid braking systems)
2	Subpar Human Narrow AI	Exhibits lower than average human intelligence or that of professionals within a very narrow domain (human-monitored self-driving cars, below average chess programs, Siri)
3	Super Human Augmented Intelligence	Exhibits superhuman artificial intelligence for narrow tasks (Alpha GO, IBM's Watson, IBM's Deep Blue)
4	Discovery AI	Level 3 AIs with the ability to interact with external AI and advertise its services, still requiring human monitoring and diligence.
5	Hands-off AGI	High level of discovery and negotiation intelligence to interact and interoperate with external AI without monitoring by humans
6	Human Governed AGI	Human regulated Artificial General Intelligence that are dynamically formed by orchestrating multiple Level 3+ AGI; able to represent humans for all tasks
7	Human Governed Artificial Super Intelligence	Human regulated Super intelligence that can excel human intelligence in all aspects and is seamlessly and effortlessly integrated with humans

In chapter 3, we discussed the chasm between the narrow AIs we see on the market today and the AGI that Bill Gates and Elon Musk are worried about. There is no bridge or clear path that shows us how we will get from where we are to one of these scary future scenarios.

The Mind-as-a-Service AI Classification nicely maps the head and tail of the AI evolution. Narrow AI like AlphaGo and Watson fit nicely a Level 3, while the Artificial General Intelligence is introduced at Level 6 and the model culminates at Level 7 with a superintelligence. Everything between Level 3 and Level 7 are the chasm that needs to be bridged.

Let's get the full picture by looking at each level of the AI evolution in more detail.

Level	Dumb Intelligence	Subpar Human Intelligence	Super Human Intelligence	Self Discovery & Negotiation	Human Governed Mind Off	Human Governed AGI	Human Governed Superintelligence
0	No	No	No	No	No	No	No
1	Yes	No	No	No	No	No	No
2	Yes	Yes	No	No	No	No	No
3	Yes	Yes	Yes	No	No	No	No
4	Yes	Yes	Yes	Yes	No	No	No
5	Yes	Yes	Yes	Yes	Yes	No	No
6	Yes	Yes	Yes	Yes	Yes	Yes	No
7	Yes	Yes	Yes	Yes	Yes	Yes	Yes

Summary of Mind-as-a-Service AI Classification. This table shows us that more sophisticated AI don't replace those at the lower levels. Rather, they enhance, supplement, or simply coexist with them.

Level 0: No Artificial Intelligence

Level 0 machines and tools are those that exhibit no human intelligence. This is the characteristic of pre-computer age technology. These technologies do enhance our abilities. The hammer extends our strength, the car improves our mobility, the telephone enhances our communication. But like forks, chopsticks, and shoes, they have zero intelligence. Those who are familiar with computer programming will recognize as basically anything that doesn't contain an "IF statement." Anything that extend our physical capabilities only, and not our intellectual abilities, is a Level 0.

Level 1: Dumb AI

Level 1 Ai are called dumb AI because they have extremely narrow and limited intellectual capabilities. It encompasses the most basic forms of automation. Calculators, for instance, enhance our cognitive abilities (if you have any doubts, just try doing complex long division by hand) but their intellectual capabilities are very limited and can't deliver significant values on their own. Yes, the calculator is indispensable when it comes to doing simple math very fast, but its scope is very small compared to a fully functional mathematical problem solver. Compared to a sophisticated math program, the calculator.

Yet another example is the thermostat: a simple senor that adjusts the temperature when it registers it below a certain range. Automation? Yes. Intelligence? Dumb, sure. Highly intelligent? Definitely not.

Level 2: Subpar Narrow AI

Level 2 MaaS AI is a Subpar Narrow AI, meaning it exhibits higher intelligence than a Level 1 AI but does not match the intelligence of an average human being. At Level 2, the human involvement is decreasing but still required because the AI simply cannot perform at a comparable level. Most of us have encountered this kind of AI in the non-playable characters in video games. Those AI have basic game intelligence – they'll follow your character or react to its actions in certain predetermined was – but most of them are simply not that good. Our current experiments with self-driving cars are attempts to program Level 2 AI. Most of the autonomous car currently on the market remain driver assisted and partially or conditionally automated, but not fully automated. These vehicles will provide some driving assistance or handle most of the driving in response to environmental cues, but a human driver still needs to perform supplementary driving tasks or take over when driving becomes too complicated (on icy roads, for instance).

Siri is another familiar example of a subpar narrow AI. Yes, it can do a lot of the things humans can, like answer natural language questions, retrieve information, or remind you of scheduled events. While it's convenient, it doesn't do anything you couldn't do, and do better. Just think about it: you might rely on Siri to keep track of an appointment or tell you the weather forecast, but would you rely on it to make life-changing decisions for you?

Level 3: Superhuman Augmented AI

A superhuman Augmented AI is an intelligence focused on one narrow task. Within our classification, a Level 3 AI is one that exhibits superhuman intelligence that "super-power" our intelligence but is devoted to a single narrow purpose. All of the artificial intelligence that currently exist are narrow AI at most, some are augmented intelligence, but most aren't.

Alpha Go and IBM's Deep Blue are good examples of superhuman narrow AI, but still not Augmented AI. Both have successfully completed tasks (games of GO and chess) in ways that surpassed human masters of those tasks. They are narrow insofar as they are restricted in their domains. A Level 3 Augmented Intelligence would be AI integrate well with human

In 2016, a speech recognition program developed by the Microsoft Artificial Intelligence and Research team was able to make the same or fewer errors than professional transcriptionists. In other words, if you hired 100 professional transcriptionists, the speech recognition program will, on average, do a better job than at least 50 of them. If the AI technologies is well integrated with a human being like a transcriptionist and become part of him or her, the result would be more significant than either just the AI or Human alone. We can also assume that it will outperform the majority of human beings since it generally outperforms those who do these tasks for a living. Another example of a Level 3 MaaS AI is the Full Automation car as defined by SAE International. Such a car could govern and drive itself without any intervention from a human driver. These cars would not even need to be designed with a steering wheel, since the car can make better driving decisions than a human, rendering the presence of a human driver entirely unnecessary.

Level 4: Discovery AI

A Level 3 MaaS AI demonstrates superhuman augmented intelligence capabilities, but each of them are restricted to their own domain. At Level 4, the AI gains active discovery and self-interoperable capabilities that allow it to integrate with one or more external Level 3 MaaS AI under human supervision. Level 4 AI have discovery mechanisms that enable them to search and negotiate AI services on their won, as well as broadcasting their capabilities as a service for hire. At this level, the AI can discover or be discovered on autopilot, but it doesn't have the ability to exercise due diligence and, therefore, still requires human monitoring. Level 4 AI are like a group of young children at the playground. Each of them is highly intelligent and can understand their environment and how to use the playground equipment. By observing older kids, they can learn how to climb up the slides and use the chain ladder. They can explore the swings and learn when to tuck in or extend their legs to get more speed. And importantly, they can seek out other kids to play with, discuss what to play, and otherwise interact with each other. Despite all these impressive capabilities and self-governing, the kids still need adult supervision because they are incapable of exercising mature judgment. Likewise, a Level 4 Mind-as-a-Service AI will be able to negotiate and interact with other AI and be rather self-governing, but it will still require some degree of human monitoring.

A real-life example of a Level 4 MaaS AI would be a fully autonomous car that has the ability to look for "driving missions" with third party AI, like an Uber algorithm that supplies driving assignments. This dynamic integration still needs to be monitored by a human because the intelligence is sophisticated enough to interact and integrate with other AI, but it doesn't have the intellectual ability to judge whether the other AI or its instructions are good. If the vehicle receives an assignment to drive to the middle of nowhere (which is highly likely to be some kind of error), the Level 4 AI would not have the intelligence to decline or question the instruction.

Of course, you can organically build a superhuman narrow AI to cover more than one domain. You could, in this case, supplement your autonomous vehicle's AI with a narrow Level 3 AI whose sole function is to evaluate driving assignments. It's at this fourth level on the MaaS AI maturity scale that we finally get to the MIA we have already discussed at length. You can allow your MIA to roam around and discover additional MIAs to collaborate with. However, it's important to remain aware of how the MIAs are interacting because at this level they do not have the intelligence to make appropriate high-level decisions.

Level 5: Hands-Off AGI

A Level 5 AI is essentially a Level 4 AI with the ability to self-govern. If the Level 4 AI are the bold children exploring the playground, Level 5 AI are their adult counterparts. It does not need to be monitored constantly or keep you up at night worried about the trouble it might get into. Level 5 AI is the point at which our MIA can do work on our behalf without our constant intervention. It's at this level that we can put it to the service of others, as discussed in Chapter 6. A Level 5,

MaaS AI is close to artificial general intelligence; however, it still only has limited general knowledge besides the ability to perform professionally in a specific niche. For example, the Level 5 AI that is able to plan your round-the-world trip won't be able to take over for you when you're preparing a meal. Likewise, it might be able to audit a major corporation but not compose poetry. Level 5 AI are still domain driven – just like us, they can master some things but they can't acquire general mastery. For that, we need a Level 6 AI.

Level 6: Human-governed Artificial General Intelligence (AGI)

A Level 6 Mind-as-a-Service AI enters the artificial general intelligence (AGI) territory with its ability to think on its own and act on your behalf based on your preferences and experience. It is like your brain on steroids. The Level 6 AGI can makes all the same decisions you are capable of making, only better.

At Level 6, the AGI is domain agnostic, meaning that it can acquire a wide range of abilities without being pigeonholed. It remains under your governance but is able to solve problems on its own. In sum, your AGI can replace you in just about any activity you perform and do it just as well as you would, if not better. If you were to give your Level 6 AGI a body, you would basically have another you.

Level 7: Human-governed Artificial General Super Intelligence (AGSI)

I include a seventh level to my Mind-as-a-Service classification because Artificial General Super Intelligence (AGSI) is held up as the holy grail and the ultimate destination of AI. In his 2014 book Superintelligence: Paths, Dangers,

Strategies, Nick Bostrom defines a Super Intelligence as "an intellect that is much smarter than the best human brains in practically every field, including scientific creativity, general wisdom and social skills." The Super Intelligence, then, outsmarts us not only intellectually, but also in its creative abilities, its predictions of the future, its invention of new solutions, and even its long-term vision, which is looks so far ahead that no human genius can fully comprehend it.

The Super Intelligence is like Genie from Disney's Aladdin, whose supernatural powers exceed any that humans could possess. He can do anything if he sets his mind to it. He is, however, magically bound by a set of obligations, mainly that he must obey and grant wishes to whoever rubs his lamp. A Level 7 Super Intelligence AI will be just like that. Like the Genie and its series of masters, control over the Super Intelligence will have to be external (in our case, in the form of government regulations). The Super Intelligence is, of course, able to outsmart us, regain complete control, and perhaps even oppose us. But I am certain that if we start our AI journey with the right vision and set of criteria in mind, we can control and govern even a Level 7 AI. We can retain the power, but we have to start now.

Conclusion

In this chapter, we have discussed in detail the Mind-as-a-Service AI classification. This system shows us how we get from the rudimentary AI that are common today to the sophisticated MIA. The map I have drawn is one that nurtures the development of human-centric AI, so that we can chart the progression of the technology without being led to doomsday scenarios in which we build increasingly complex forms of artificial intelligence only to be taken over by them.

The next part of the book will address that last concern more directly. In it, we will focus on the core idea of the book, namely, how to tame artificial intelligence.

171

PART 6

TAMING ARTIFICIAL INTELLIGENCE

CHAPTER 12
AI GOVERNANCE & REGULATIONS

AI is a rare case where we need to be proactive about regulation instead of reactive. Because I think by the time we are reactive in AI regulation, it's too late.
— Elon Musk

In this chapter, you will learn about:
• The need for regulation
• AI regulations
• AI governance
• Implementing regulations and governance

What is the ethical nature of Artificial Intelligence algorithms? Are they good? Are they evil? Are they neutral? Do we need to worry about them hating – and turning against –

humans?

We don't know the answer yet. No one does. It's a question that has been asked repeatedly since artificial intelligence was first conceived. There seems to be little hope of making a firm prediction on the matter. Philosophers have debated human morality for thousands of years, after all, and have yet to come to a consensus on whether we are good by nature and corrupted by society, or naturally selfish and kept in check by social pressures. My own personal opinion (and not an official element of the Mind-as-a-Service model) is that the majority of humans (those whose brain wiring makes them psychopathic or sociopathic are notable exceptions) are inheritably good. Unless we face a serious conflict of interests, most of us will not put ourselves first in a way that brings harm to others. As a framework, Mind-as-a-Service doesn't take an official position on whether AI is bad in nature or whether it has any intention to cause harm. It does, however, acknowledge that there is a risk that AI could put us in harm's way. This wouldn't necessarily result from any ill intention on the part of the AI; humans could simply be collateral damage sustained by the AI trying to achieve whatever goal it has.

We have spent much of the book discussing the capabilities and classifications of MaaS AI. We've looked over the promise of the Mind-as-a-Service model: that we can build incredibly powerful artificial intelligence agents without being taken over by them. But throughout, we have alluded to the importance of regulation. For the proliferation of advanced AI to be a net benefit to our species, its development and use will have to be constrained and controlled to some extent. In this chapter, we will look at this need for regulation and governance in greater detail.

We are still in the very early phase of AI development. Most of the program on the market are automations or subpar artificial intelligences, such as software with machine learning processes. These are rudimentary advances compared to what is coming in the foreseeable future, but its effects have been huge. Currently available AI have been effective and productive in helping us do a lot more with a lot less. We're already seeing how automation can free us up from making every single decision and spending time doing low-level, repetitive work. We've also seen a number of promising prototypes for products that should soon be commonly available on the market. Self-driving cars and chatbots have done impressive things, and they will soon use their abilities to make life easier for the average consumer. We do have a smattering of superhumanly intelligent machines developed by tech giants like IBM, Google, and Microsoft, but not many of these are available, nor is it always clear hwo they will be commercialized (Watson is an impressive machine, but few of us will be willing to spend huge sums just to bring our personal Watson to trivia night at the bar). These developments seem geared more toward enterprise-level AI, which are built at corporate scale and used to handle business processes.

Our legislation is not advancing at the same pace as our technological developments. Self-driving cars will soon be ready for mass manufacturing, but it's not entirely clear how law-makers will react. Super-intelligent AI may soon become a part of the corporate world, using its advanced abilities to increase profit and maximize shareholder value, but they might be ushered in with only the thin regulations that barely restrain human corporate actors. With all of these advances comes some risk, and the right way to react to them will depend strongly on the level and type of risk we are facing. It's worth, then, looking more closely as the concept of risk before discussing ways to manage it.

Risk

Risk is the chance that something or someone might become exposed to harm or loss. The risk of investing in stock market, for example, is the chance that the investor will lose their money if the market goes south. Likewise, anyone starting a business runs the risk of running into too many expenses with too little revenue to make up for it.

The Mind-as-a-Service framework acknowledges that there are risks in developing advanced AI. Because of this, it has mechanisms to mitigate the risks. Before we look at how MaaS proposes to minimize risk, let's discuss the need for regulation.

Drugs

The U. S. Food and Drug Administration is the oldest federal agency dedicated to consumer protection. It is a scientific, regulatory, and public health agency that oversees items that collective account for 25 percent of consumer spending. Its jurisdiction encompasses most food products (other than meat and poultry), human and animal drugs, therapeutic agents of biological origin, medical devices, radiation-emitting products for consumer and professional use, cosmetics, and animal feed. Originally a single chemist appointed to the U. S. Department of Agriculture in 1862, the FDA has grown substantially, starting with the passage of the Pure Food and Drugs Act in 1906. Now, the FDA employs more than 10,000 chemists, pharmacologists, physicians, microbiologists, pharmacists, veterinarians, lawyers, and other experts, powered by a $1.83 billion budget.

The challenge of providing the American public with safe and effective medication has grown in concert with the expansion of the drug armamentarium over the last century. This expansion in treatment methods has, unfortunately, not been an unimpeded march of progress and improvement to human health. In fact, changes in the way drugs are regulated have usually been born out of tragic events with large numbers of casualties.

Before the 20th century, powerful substances were traded and used with very little oversight. Now-notorious drugs like cocaine were used rather casually, often in over-the-counter pharmaceutical products. In 1906, the federal government took a leap forward in controlling the use and sale of these products by instituting the Pure Food and Drugs Act. This law prohibited interstate commerce in adulterated or misbranded drugs and made the United States Pharmacopoeia and the National Formulary the official standards for drugs. It also required product labels to list the presence and amount of some dangerous and addictive ingredients, such as alcohol, morphine, heroin, and cocaine. This rather tame labeling law (although it was a vast improvement over the underregulated Wild West drug market that preceded it) was enhanced in 1938 with an FDA ruling that some drugs were simply too dangerous to be considered safe for mass commercial use, regardless of their dosage. By 1941, more than 20 drugs or drug groups now could only be distributed with a prescription from a certified medical professional, including sulfas, barbiturates, and amphetamines.

Drugs have incredible benefits, and we are fortunate to live in a time in which they can be used to alleviate discomfort and pain, treat serious illness, and prolong life. But they all come with risks, sometimes very grave ones. Uneducated, uninformed, and unregulated use of drugs can turn these life-saving and beneficial medications into dangerous and harmful substances. We should be grateful that we no longer live at the dawn of the drug regulation or have to suffer through its slow, decades-long progression.

Let's imagine that we have never made the slow but steady progress. What would a world without drug regulation look like? It would be convenient in some ways: we could buy any drug we need, from anti-depressants to radioactive chemotherapy treatments, right from off the shelf at our local Walmart.

But that utopian vision of unrestricted access has a dark side to it. Adolescence is a time of high emotions that are difficult to control and often challenging to cope with. With anti-depressants available over the counter there's no doubt that some high school kids will start taking them to cope with everything from trouble at school to parents scolding the. They quickly become the easy road to happiness, and without any way to regulate teenagers' intake (their supply will be as big as their pockets are deep), we would like see a wave of addiction. And what about chemotherapy drugs? Could its radioactive components be extracted by those who want to use them to make dangerous weapons or dirty bombs? And without regulation, we also have a problem on the supply side. Just about anyone could mix chemicals or boil herbs at home, and then throw it out of the market with wild claims about its abilities to cure AIDS or cancer. We'd still be in the era of snake oil salesmen, only this time the snake oil could do a lot more harm than a placebo.

Guns

Canada's history of gun regulations can also prove instructive. While American laws have generally protected the right for civilians to own and use firearms, there is a very different history of gun control north of the border. Canadian control over civilian use of firearms dates from the early days of Confederation, when justices of the peace could impose penalties to anyone carrying a handgun without reasonable cause. Amendments to the Criminal Code between the 1890s and the 1970s introduced a series of additional minor controls on firearms, but major restrictions were introduced in the mid-1990s These regulations either reflect or influence Canadian culture – fewer than 3% of Canadian households had handguns in 2005, compared to 18% of American households.

Guns are powerful tools that extend our ability to apply deadly force from a long distance. A gun by itself won't hurt anyone, but once it's in the hands of a human being, it will significantly increase the odds of someone becoming gravely injured. Regulation matters in this context because of the potential devastation of misusing firearms. Like guns, knives and blunt items can be used to inflict deadly wounds, but the careless use of a firearm is more likely to have devastating consequences.

Military grade weaponry is regulated much more strictly

than conventional firearms. And while there are some who may be disappointed that they can't spend a weekend driving a tank around their backyard or firing mortar shells in their backyard like they were fireworks, it's safe to say most of us prefer to live in a world where we can't drive off the car dealership in a tank or rent a stealth bomber from the local airfield.

Regulations cannot stop every villainous person from causing serious harm. After all, prohibited firearms still make their way into the hands of domestic terrorists, people committing armed robbery can do it by using hunting rifles and other licensed weapons, and once a legal firearm is sold it is difficult to prevent its owner from illegally modifying it. Still, regulations can control risks to some extent, as we can see by the different rates of gun ownership in Canada and America, corresponding to the strength of the regulations in each country.

Alcohol

Alcohol is also a dangerous item, but one that is consumed recreationally. It is regulated, but like firearms there are discrepancies across the 49th parallel. Most notably, the legal drinking age in America is 21, while Canadians can legally purchase alcohol at age 18 or 19 (depending on the province).

Alcohol is regulated because we know it can be harmful to human health. But what makes it different than, say, junk food? For one, alcohol can have adverse effects on the developing brain and body (hence prohibiting sales of it to children and adolescents across North America). It also has behavioral effects that are dangerous for those who haven't achieved a certain level of maturity. The loss of self-control and inhibition that comes along with intoxication can lead to terrible decision-making for children who have yet to learn how to properly judge risks or adolescents who have yet to appreciate the consequences of risky behavior. Of course, age is only an approximate measure of maturity, and all of us know at least one adult who is too poor a judge to responsibly consume alcohol, but the age restriction at least limits the risks associated with alcohol (or at the very least, attempts to restrict consumption to those who are legally responsible for their conduct). Age restriction is only one of the regulations, of course. Bars are prohibited from serving drinks to someone who has had too much and driving under the influence of alcohol is something that can get you in trouble with the law.

The Dangers of AI

Unlike the chemical substances (drugs, poison, alcohol, herbs) and mechanical devices (cars, guns, heavy machines) we discussed so far, AI has the ability to make its own decisions. A parked car won't cause anyone harm, but an AI-driven one could because it has its own ability to turn on the ignition and drive off, or even open a door when a cyclist is riding next to it. When we move through the MaaS AI classifications from the simple, narrow AI that we currently make use of to the superintelligences and artificial general intelligences that will be a big part of our future, will we want to leave our fate in the hands of machines that have no limits on the exercise of their capabilities?

But how can we predict the level of risk we are going to face? With pharmaceuticals, firearms, and alcohol, we have the benefit of hindsight: we became quite familiar with the risks associated with them before legislators imposed controls on their use. But it's different with artificial intelligence. We can't simply look at how thermostats (a "dumb" AI) have changed our lives and use it to gauge the risks associated with superintelligent machines. Here, we have to dip into the toolkit of philosophers and fiction authors and try to imagine the kinds of scenarios we could face in the future.

Let's start by considering an enterprise AI called David. David was created by a multinational enterprise to maximize profits for its shareholders, mainly by reducing costs and inefficiencies. But based on its analyses, David has determined that one of the best approaches to maximize profitability is to eliminate competitors. So, David starts considering various options for eliminating the competition and determines that the easiest way is to order the company's fleet of trucks to ram into the major competitors' factories in order to cause heavy damage and slow their production. Refusal from truck drivers is no problem; the company moved to fully automated trucks a few years prior. By the time anyone at the company finds out about David's plan, it will already have been carried out. Of course, there are liability issues to consider, not to mention court costs and a possible hitch in insurance premiums, but David can factor all those in and decide whether the benefits outweigh the costs.

And David is not finished. When it looks at the human capital expenses listed on the balance sheet, it realizes that this is the costliest item. Without the fully formed judgment that allows it to carefully consider the quality of each individual worker, David goes for an efficient route: firing all employees with high salaries and replacing them with less experienced employees with entry-level salaries. To David, the decision just makes sense, but it doesn't take a business expert to realize that this move will be devastating to the company.

You may say that all this happens because David's thinking is too narrow and doesn't fully appreciate liability, talent management, and a lot of common sense. I don't disagree, but how can we know that David has all the relevant kinds of knowledge and intelligence we send it out to do what it was built to do? There's no foolproof way – since David is highly intelligent, it's impossible to test all possible outcomes. Indeed, that's why self-driving cars that have travelled millions of miles without causing any accidents are still not deemed ready for commercial use. The real world is extremely complex, and even after traveling those millions of miles, automated vehicles have not encountered every scenario they will face once they hit public streets.

David is not built with the intention to hurt people. In fact, he is designed specifically to bring value. Yet it may cause harm simply because it lacks certain aspects of common sense, or it doesn't have the ability to balance complex sets of considerations when making weighing decisions. David is like a highly intelligent teenager: extremely clever, but not yet fully wise to the way the world works. Like a clever teenager, the best solution to ensure that David doesn't make some terrible decision is to give him some adult supervision in the form of human monitoring. . David needs rules, limits, and should have some of its major decisions checked by humans. In other words, David and other sophisticated AI need governance. And if that governance isn't just the AI's owner keeping tabs on it, but involves enforcement by government bodies, then we will refer to it as AI regulation.

Up until now, we have painted a fairly positive picture by only discussing AI built with good intentions, like David. But what about AI that are created for the express purpose of bringing harm to people? AI is a powerful tool and all sectors will want to exploit it, and that includes military and law enforcement. But it can also fall into the wrong hands. So, consider the following scenario. Dominic is an AI created by a military enterprise that supplies weapons to terrorist organizations. Dominic's goal is to benefit the arms dealer financially, using whatever means and method are needed. So, Dominic initiates Project T, which consists of a midterm strategy to promote wars between countries whose conflict would be advantageous to the enterprise, mainly by encouraging the warring factions to buy weaponry from them. Project T initiates a fake news engine to spread propaganda and rumors, injecting paranoia and distrust in already tense political relationships. Fabricated news reports pour in that each country is building up its armories, and the governments respond in turn by increasing military spending in preparation for a coming war. Dominic succeeds in its task – the ensuing arms race enriches the weapons dealer on a scale it never saw before.

A science fiction scenario? In part, but there are some worrisome precedents. Facebook, now a major source of news for many citizens, is awash with misleading headlines, fake reports, and photoshopped images passing as documentary evidence. With a superintelligent AI pulling the levers behind the curtains, how long before this kind of misinformation could cause a missile to be launched, initiating an unwarranted but quite deadly conflict?

AI Governance & Regulation

A highly intelligence and autonomous AI is more dangerous than the most harmful substances in the world, more dangerous than the heaviest machinery we've developed, and could possibly cause more damage than some of our deadliest weapons. Indeed, part of its danger lies in the fact that the AI can orchestrate, manipulate, and make use of all of these harmful things in strategic ways.

AI governance and regulation is a solution to these potential risks. It's too soon to quantify the risk, and I won't stake my entire reputation on a prediction, but I think it's safe to assume that unrestricted AI development poses a medium to high threat.

Like regulations that govern our use of drugs, alcohol, weapons, and heavy machinery, AI regulations can provide clear guidelines to the general public, clearly outlining what is considered acceptable and unacceptable when it comes to building and using AI.

Advantages of AI Governance & Regulation

There are a few advantages in regulating AI – some obvious and direct, others less so. I won't run the entire gamut of benefits here, but it's worthwhile to pause briefly and consider what we stand to gain from taking these important steps.

Regulation, for one thing, will mobilize campaigns that seek to communicate with the public and educate them about the dangers of misusing AI or developing dangerous technologies. As AI becomes an ordinary commodity, these educational campaigns will be essential. Similar educational campaigns about the risks associated with alcohol have been quite successful. Thanks to successful advocacy from groups such as M.A.D.D., young people all grow up knowing the dangers of drunk driving, and it's an activity that has become highly stigmatized. Running comparable campaigns about the dangers of AI could lead to widespread awareness of AI safety and best practices.

The main advantage of AI regulation, however, will be the ability to put a stop to business operations or close it down entirely if it is found in violation in its use or development of AI. Companies that try to rush an autonomous vehicle to market before it is fully tested for safety or who work on an AI that will violate traffic laws so that it can deliver goods more quickly can be stopped before their products put people at risk.

Regulation does admittedly have its drawbacks. The first that comes to mind is cost. There's a far lower sticker price to letting corporations develop whatever AI they please and not spending resources policing private uses of AI. Like all forms of compliance, it will take a cost not only on the regulatory bodies (the government agencies who will have to find ways to enforce regulation within its budgetary constraints) but the companies that build the AI as well. These corporations will require the services of specialized lawyers and software engineers to ensure that the AI algorithm conforms to all existing laws.

Governing and Regulating Intelligence Is Nothing New

If this seems like a heavy-handed approach, it's important to realize that this is not the first time we've taken steps to regulate intelligence. In fact, even human intelligence is regulated. No, nobody is going to shut down our brains if we misuse them, but there are restrictions on what we legally allowed to do with our intellectual capabilities. For instance, we are not permitted to lie under oath, or scam people out of their life savings by exploiting their trustworthiness.

When to Regulate

The best time to introduce AI regulations is before the AI becomes a risk. As we've seen above, the real world rarely works this way. Substances and devices have usually only become regulated once they've caused quite a fair bit of harm. Unfortunately, that harm is often a precondition for public support: until we see widespread harm from unregulated AI, the public may not be keen on tax dollars being spent regulating their newest gadgets, especially since the companies that create them are likely to engage in extensive media campaigns to convince users that AI is extremely safe.

The power of AI is far too complex and unforeseeable, however. We don't have the luxury of waiting. Deciding to "cross that bridge when we get there" would be irresponsible. For one thing, if regulation comes too late, companies may have already sunk millions or billions into developing AI that they must then shut down once the government finally decides to impose restrictions.

That, however, would be a better scenario than the alternative: waiting so long that these companies do release their unregulated AI on the open market. Who knows what could happen and who could get hurt when these powerful products are released into the wild.

I understand the need for prudence and caution when it comes to legislation, and it's important in general to avoid overregulation (if there was one lesson we can learn from the prohibition era, it's that being overly restrictive will quickly lose popular support).

So, when is the best time to start regulating AI?

The right time to start discussing regulation is now. I don't mean regulating the AI that we already have out there – I'm not suggesting that we start drafting laws to govern the use of Nest thermostats. What I mean is we should be prepared. We need to have the regulation ready and in place before we reach a point where the regulations are too little and too late. Once AI horse is out the stable, it won't do much good to close the door. AI can grow and learn at an exceptional rate, and its rate of self-improvement could be exponential. Unlike an auto engine, which could take years or decades to get from its 200 mile-per-hour limit to speeds that can reach 400 miles-per-hour, a sufficiently autonomous AI could double its capabilities in a matter of days or even hours.

On Oct 18, 2017, Google's Deep Mind released a report declaring that their latest version of Alpha GO, AlphaGO Zero, can learn to play GO on its own, without having the rules and strategies programmed into it ahead of time. It has, moreover, become the best GO player in just 21 days, beating the world's GO champion, Ke Jie, in three out of three games, as well as 60 professional GO players). 21 days is all it takes for an AI to go from knowing absolutely nothing about the game to mastering it to a superhuman degree. And this is only 2017. Who knows what kind of AI enhancements will come our way in the next few years.

To summarize, my main points are that:

1.   AI moves faster than regulation tends to move.

2.   So, we should start drafting regulations before we usher in the next generation of AI capabilities.

3.   Because if we wait too late and some AI run amok, bringing about large-scale harm, we will face chaos that is

extremely difficult to contain.

Levels of Regulations

If we are going regulate AI, where should we start? I propose that we start by drawing up a classification system that is similar to the ones we use for other harmful substances. Some drugs, for example, are classified as over-the-counter (unrestricted), some require a prescription, while others are flat out illegal. Likewise, some firearms can be obtained with a license, while others are not legally available to civilians. We can draw the same kinds of distinctions and nuances with AI, too.

In Chapter 11, I introduced the Mind-as-a-Service classification system.

Level	Dumb Intelligence	Subpar Human Intelligence	Super Human Intelligence	Self Discovery & Negotiation	Human Governed Mind Off	Human Governed AGI	Human Governed Superintelligence
0	No	No	No	No	No	No	No
1	Yes	No	No	No	No	No	No
2	Yes	Yes	No	No	No	No	No
3	Yes	Yes	Yes	No	No	No	No
4	Yes	Yes	Yes	Yes	No	No	No
5	Yes	Yes	Yes	Yes	Yes	No	No
6	Yes	Yes	Yes	Yes	Yes	Yes	No
7	Yes	Yes	Yes	Yes	Yes	Yes	Yes

This can serve as a basic template for regulation. The higher up we move on the scale, the stricter the regulations will need to be. I won't attempt to come up with the exact details here, but it's likely that Level 4, where superintelligence is introduced, is where we should start putting in significant restrictions. A superintelligent AI like AlphaGO Zero might not cause much harm (though there's no telling how upset Ke Jie was to be defeated by a machine), but a similar AI that is tasked with, say, flying a drone could easily violate someone's privacy, leak sensitive information (if it is equipped with some kind of recording device), or physically hurt someone by crashing into them.

As I said, I won't attempt to draft a robust set of regulations. But it would be a worthwhile exercise for politicians and legislators to engage in before we reach higher levels on the MaaS scale and aren't prepared to deal with its realities.

Liability

In discussions of regulation, the question of liability always come up. Who is liable if some AI violates the rules? Is it the AI itself since it can act autonomously, the way AlphaGO Zero taught itself to play the game? And if so, do we issue a fine to the AI's owner or do we shut it down the way a dog to sleep if it attacks someone?

Or is the company that manufacture the AI liable? It's plausible, but then again we don't fine or sue Toyota when someone drives one of their trucks into the crowd. So would we hold the manufacturer liable if the autonomous vehicle that taught itself to drive didn't recognize pedestrians crossing the street?

These issues will have to be worked out. The philosopher Thomas Hobbes wrote that making something illegal without attaching any punishment to the violation is essentially the same as making it permissible. If no one is held accountable, and there are no serious consequences for some party when the AI causes harm, then there will be nothing holding either the AI, its developers, or its owners responsible.

The Solution: Human-Centric AI Regulation

One of the many beauties of the Mind-as-a-Service framework is that it makes the humans who use the AI responsible and accountable for it. The framework is human-centric, meaning that all uses of the AI need to benefit human beings. If a self-driving car mows down a crowd of pedestrians ¬– hardly a human-centric act! – the owner will be held liable for it.

Is this a fair solution? Since we don't have full control over the AI, how is it that we are held accountable for its decisions? The question rests on a mistaken assumption. We do have some control over our AI. The AI grows and learns under our guidance and according to our commands; it is up to us to prevent it from going rogue.

In the world of Mind-as-a-Service, the chain of responsibility runs something like the following.

Governments define the regulation, and certain AI have to be certified or tested, the way cars are.

Manufacturers are required to have all of their AI certified under government monitoring before their products are released onto the market.

Design flaws and malfunctions will fall on the manufacturer's shoulders. But when it comes to how far an AI is pushed or what purpose it is used for, the responsibility will solely be that of the owner or the user.

Think of it as buying a car from the dealership. The manufacturer is responsible for the car's design and function (that's why the manufacturer will issue a recall at their own expense if its products are found defective), while the buyer is responsible for what happens when they're driving the car or deciding to park it in a certain location.

Similarly, adopting a dog gives you a number of responsibilities, even if you cannot fully control the dog. There are reasonable measures you can take to apply control – a leash, a muzzle, training classes, or simply keeping the dog fenced in at home. Regardless of the measures you put in place, at the end of the day if your dog bites someone, you are held accountable. Your dog may be put down if it's deemed dangerous, and you may be issued a fine or some other form of punishment if you are found to have been negligent in your capacity as the dog's owner.

The line between an AI and a human is blurring, but with a Mind-as-a-Service approach, all AI are considered extensions of human intelligence. So, all of the AI's activities are jointly held to be the responsibility of both the AI and the human whose intelligence is extended through it. The AI may be easily shut down (unlike the dog in the previous example, it thankfully has no feelings), but it is the human user who is held responsible, whether it's the consumer of the AI or the supervisor or director of the company that makes use of it.

CHAPTER 13
TAMING ARTIFICIAL INTELLIGENCE

"The path from dreams to success does exist. May you have the vision to find it, the courage to get on to it, and the perseverance to follow it."-Kalpana Chawla

We have come to the last chapter of book. I have given it the same name as the book itself – Taming Artificial Intelligence. When trying to come up with a title for the book, I worked through many options but finally settled on this one because I want to convey the fact that I don't consider AI to be in competition with us. Instead, I think of it more as an outsider species in a state of infancy. We know the new species will be superior to us at some point, but at this stage they simply aren't very smart and they're well under our control. However, as they develop, they continue to surprise us with their improved abilities. These are abilities that we can harness for our benefit if we take a careful and considered approach to our relationship with this species. They are growing powerful, butw e can envision a world in which the AI can help us, work for us, and obey us.

This is unprecedented. We have encountered countless other species before, and we have lived alongside or worked with many of them to our benefit. We don't, however, expect any of them to evolve to the point where they surpass our intelligence. And if we can envision a kind of Planet of the Apes scenario, it certainly won't happen in our lifetime, or even our grandchildren's lifetimes.

Our encounters with AI are unprecedented and that is precisely why we need to get in the right relationship with it now. We have never had to deal with a role reversal like the one that is coming. At some point, at least if we're young enough, we will live in a world where we are no longer the most intelligent species. Artificially intelligent machines will be the pinnacle of intelligence, with us at a distant second. We need to prepare for this future and do so in a way that ensures that we regain control, even when we cease being the most intelligent entities on the planet.

Taming the Beast

Mind-as-a-Service is a framework for taming the new species. Before they turn against us, we need to make sure they are domesticated. We have done that with dogs and cats, but we have had time to do so gradually, over countless years. We will have to accelerate the process with our approach to AI.

I think of AI as a human extension. As such, I want to tame them to make sure we are all on the same team. AI have no souls, no feelings – they are simply machines and we have no obligations to them. It is not unreasonable to demand their total and utter subservience to human needs and interests.

There's a well-worn saying that you can't teach an old dog new tricks. Accordingly, we tame a beast while it's still a cub. We need to take the same approach with AI. If left to its own devices, it will learn and develop in whatever direction it sees fit. We need to gain control over it before it becomes an old dog.

Sun Wukong again

In Chapter 5, I relayed the story of Sun Wukong, the Monkey King. Five hundred years after Sun Wukong made a mess in the Heavenly Kingdom and was captured by Buddha, the Bodhisattva Guanyin searches for disciples to protect a pilgrim on a journey to the West to retrieve the Buddhist sutras. When he hears word of this, Sun Wukong offers to serve the pilgrim, Xuanzang, a monk of the Tang dynasty, in exchange for his freedom after the pilgrimage is complete. Knowing that the monkey will be difficult to control, Guanyin gives Xuanzang a gift from the Buddha: a magical headband which, once Sun Wukong is tricked into putting it on, can never be removed. A special spell will cause the headband to tighten, giving the monkey king an unbearable headache.

Like Xuanzang, we all wish to have powerful allies in our own journeys. A powerful ally, however, can be a double edge sword. They can help you, but if they turn against you, you might be powerless to stop them. Xuanzang was in that position, but he had a foolproof mechanism – the magical headband – that offered him peace of mind. It's important for us to have these kinds of mechanisms in place for our AI. If it malfunctions, acts funny, or makes us miserable in any way, we need the ability to do something about it. It's a drastic step, so not one that we would want to exercise without good reason. But it's better to be safe than sorry, and without these kinds of mechanisms in place, we will inevitably be sorry.

Labor or Capital?

Considering AI as extensions of our abilities rather than as our competitors has other advantages. If AI are independent entities that compete with us for our job, they are a form of labor. When their labor power is pitted against ours, we won't have much to offer to an employer that an AI cannot supply or exceed.

If, on the other hand, AI are extensions of our abilities, they will be a form of capital that we own. They will, in other words, be an investment that we make in order to get a higher rate of return on the effort we put into our work. To upgrade and equip our MaaS AI is to invest in ourselves, not to strengthen a competitor. Rather than stealing our jobs and leaving us destitute, the AI-as-capital acts as our safety net and becomes our path to retirement.

Our AI can allow us to be always on without requiring our constant attention. It can continue to work for us when we are having lunch, taking our kids to school, or sunbathing on a beach in the Caribbean. AI will replace real estate and stocks as our most valuable investments. We will not only invest in in the stock market, but also in our AI and even other people's AI, hoping to claim a share of their AI's success. We may also crowdsource our AI investment, selling shares of our AI and letting investors purchase a piece of its productivity.

However the AI manifests itself as capital, one thing is for certain: the world will be a very different place than it is today.

The Human-AI evolution will be slow, steady, and fruitful

The AI evolution will be millions of years faster than natural human evolution, but it will nevertheless be stable, steady, and much slower than a Revolution. By definition, a revolution is a sudden and extreme change of events that has a significant impact on the way people live and work. That won't be the case for AI. It won't cause such a sudden disruption because it won't reach that point in its evolution (say level 5 or higher on the Mind-as-a-Service AI Classification scale) anytime soon. And by the time we reach that point, AI will already be a part of us.

As you can tell from reading this book, I am very optimistic about the future of AI, and very excited that our generation is fortunate enough to participate in this incredible opportunity. We are the first humans who will actually be able to speed up our evolution. There will be unforeseen risks and challenges, but we will be prepared.

ABOUT THE AUTHOR

Brian Ka Chan is a futuristic technology strategist who helps for-profit, government, and non-profit organizations ("Tri-athletes" Professional) to maximize productivity through intelligent automation, data and analytics, and the latest digital technologies. Brian's ambition is to help individuals achieve the same improved productivity with inevitable advancement of artificial intelligence and smart machines.

Brian holds a Master's Degree in Computer Engineering from the University of Toronto and a Bachelor of Science degree in Electrical and Computer Engineering from Queen's University, Canada.

Brian has two decades of experience in innovation strategic planning, data transformation, and technology architecture.

He is currently the Managing Director of Mind Data (MindData.org) focuses on next generation Technologies, based in Toronto, Canada. Brian has helped Fortune 500 technology companies to create next generation commercial products using data, digital, and intelligent automation technologies.

199

200